THE BEST
STEAMBOAT
HIKES

JACQUELYNE COX

The Colorado Mountain Club Press
Golden, Colorado

The Best Steamboat Hikes
© 2017 by The Colorado Mountain Club

All rights reserved. No part of this publication may be reproduced or transmitted in any form or by any means, electronic or mechanical, including photocopy, recording, or by any information storage and retrieval system without permission in writing from the publisher.

PUBLISHED BY

The Colorado Mountain Club Press
710 Tenth Street, Suite 200, Golden, Colorado 80401
303-996-2743   email: cmcpress@cmc.org
website: http://www.cmc.org

Founded in 1912, The Colorado Mountain Club is the largest outdoor recreation, education, and conservation organization in the Rocky Mountains. Look for our books at your local bookstore or outdoor retailer or online at www.cmc.org/books.

CONTACTING THE PUBLISHER
We would appreciate it if readers would alert us to any errors or outdated information by contacting us at the above address.

Jacquelyne Cox, author, photographer
Takeshi Takahashi: design, composition, and production
Melanie K. Stafford: copy editor
Clyde Soles: publisher

DISTRIBUTED TO THE BOOK TRADE BY
Mountaineers Books, 1001 Klickitat Way, Suite 201, Seattle, WA 98134, 800-553-4453, www.mountaineersbooks.org

COVER PHOTO: Flat Top Mountain as seen from Devil's Causeway. Photo by Jacquelyne Cox

We gratefully acknowledge the financial support of the people of Colorado through the Scientific and Cultural Facilities District of greater Denver for our publishing activities.

TOPOGRAPHIC MAPS were created using CalTopo.com.

WARNING: Although there has been an effort to make the trail descriptions in this book as accurate as possible, some discrepancies may exist between the text and the trails in the field. Hiking in mountain areas is a high-risk activity. This guidebook is not a substitute for experience and common sense. The users of this guidebook assume full responsibility for their own safety. Weather, terrain conditions, and individual abilities must be considered before undertaking any of the hikes in this guide.

ISBN: 978-1-937052-48-5

Gilpin Lake

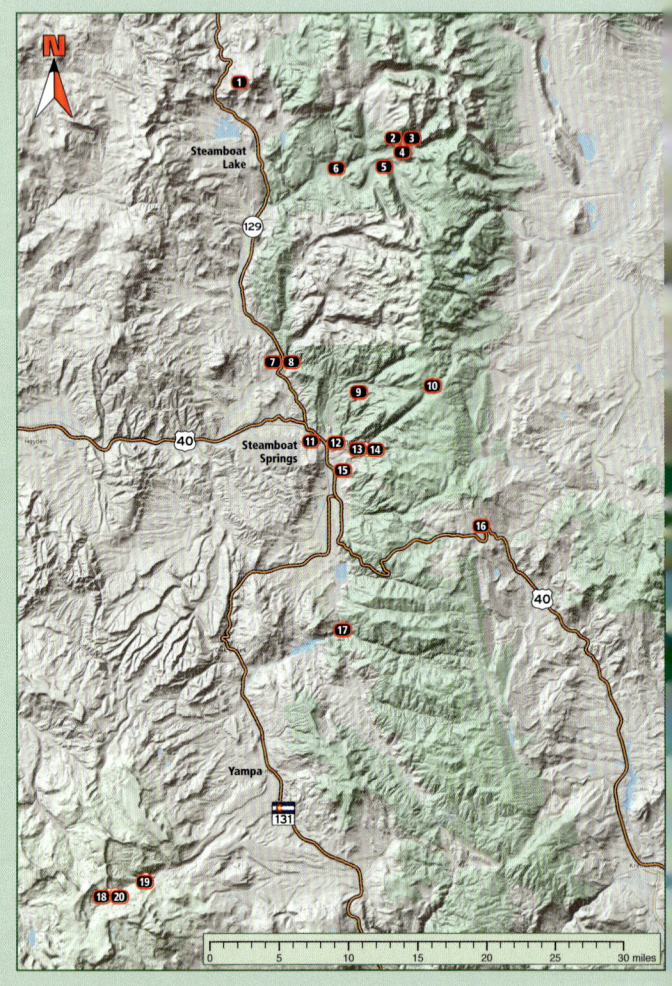

OVERVIEW MAP

CONTENTS

Acknowledgments 6
Introduction 8
The Ten Essentials 11
Wildlife Viewing Tips 13

THE HIKES

1. Hahns Peak 14
2. Mica Basin 18
3. Gold Creek Lake/Zirkel Circle 24
4. Gilpin Lake 30
5. Three Island Lake 34
6. Hinman Lake 38
7. Mad Creek and Saddle Trail 42
8. Strawberry Park Hot Springs Hike 46
9. Soda Creek 50
10. Grizzly Lake 54
11. Emerald Mountain Quarry/Blackmere ... 58
12. Spring Creek 62
13. Uranium Mine 66
14. Fish Creek Falls/Upper Fish Creek Falls ... 70
15. Thunderhead Trail 74
16. Rabbit Ears Peak 78
17. Sarvis Creek 82
18. Devil's Causeway 88
19. Mandall Lakes Trail/Mandall Pass 94
20. Flat Top Mountain 100

About the Author 106
Checklist 107

ACKNOWLEDGMENTS

This is a different acknowledgment of sorts because I am lucky and so very thankful to be here in the first place, to be able to write, to have a conscious thought, to speak, to see, or even to walk. In the spring of 2015, I was to relocate to Steamboat from Vail. My things were packed, and the moving truck was scheduled for May 1. It had been in the making almost a year as it was, to finally move to the place I knew I belonged.

At the same time, after experiencing a number of mysterious symptoms for months and being too stubborn to see a doctor about them, I reached a tipping point and had to be taken to the emergency room in the Vail Valley. An MRI revealed lesions on my brain. Finally, after weeks of testing in Denver, I was diagnosed with encephalitis—a rare yet serious illness involving inflammation of the brain. There were so many unknowns because the outcome is specific to each individual case. Would I get my vision back? What about my balance and coordination? I couldn't write with a pencil, my speech was slurred, and I stuttered and/or couldn't think of the right words. I had no short-term memory. I wasn't allowed to walk without assistance.

This was a journey in its own right, one that I never anticipated. I was unsure of the outcome, as were my family and friends. I endured a brutal summer and fall of treatment and concoctions of prescription drugs, living in a shell of a home surrounded by boxes and disorganization; I was too weak to unpack my things, let alone walk upstairs. I was unable to appreciate my new home and the surroundings that I so cherished. But I was determined to get through this, and day by day, month by month, very slowly, I recovered.

Fast forward to when the opportunity of writing a hiking guidebook for Steamboat came my way in the spring of 2016. Science is still coming to a conclusion about this, but I have no doubt that hiking is beneficial for brain health. And I could not think of a better way to finally get to know the area I love surrounding my home, and to celebrate life, and all the little things we tend to take for granted.

To my family and friends, your support, kind words, and encouragement gave me strength each and every day; I am forever grateful. I'd like to thank my physical and occupational therapists at Sports Med. To my very patient and understanding doctor, Jennifer Kempers, at Yampa Valley Medical Center, your continued guidance was reassuring. To my friend Ty Upson, thank you for sharing your formidable knowledge of the area and for loaning me your space as I completed hikes in and around North Routt. To Charlie Noble and the friends I've made while moonlighting at Mahogany Ridge because I needed my daytimes free, thank you for the laughs and humor as I hiked my way through the summer and fall. And most importantly, I'd like to thank Director of Publishing Clyde Soles of Colorado Mountain Club Press and a longtime friend and colleague. I give him sincere thanks and gratitude for trusting me with this opportunity and to be able to share these hikes with all of you.

Üllr enjoying the flowers near Grizzly Lake.

I dedicate this book to Mom, Dad and to a few special friends, the most innocent and sentient of beings, my pups past and present. To those who have passed on—Moab, Shadow, Beauregard, Ruger—I am so grateful to have had you at my side through some of the most fun, poignant, and changing times in my life. And to my sweet companion Üllr; at thirteen years old you have been a pillar of support, helping me overcome a serious illness more than a year and a half ago. I am so grateful you were able to accompany me on several hikes in this book. I love you, buddy, and long may you run.

Introduction

The Yampa Valley, home to Steamboat Springs, is a very special and unique place. One needs to hike only a mile or two up Emerald Mountain to see the valleys firsthand, long and wide, with sweeping mountain ranges surrounding them all around, the town sitting in the center of it all with big open skies above and the Yampa River bringing life to it all. Unlike many other regions in Colorado, there aren't any 14ers, mountains over 14,000 feet high, which are a popular draw for many to hike and check off their "bucket list." One needs to go no farther than the Zirkels for a true alpine experience with tall, craggy peaks and blue lakes. With the unprecedented growth Colorado has seen, especially over the past few years, it's important to many to find a place with more room to spread out and explore; Steamboat offers this. The best part is all of the wonderful people that make up this great place. At the end of the day, we are not just a world-class destination resort; we are a community first and foremost.

Steamboat sits just to the northwest of the Continental Divide, and in the winter we (usually) get blessed with an overabundance of snow. You may have heard the phrase "come for the winters, stay for the summers"; though the summers are short, I think Steamboat is just that place. In the spring and early summer when everything melts, the landscape takes on a lush green hue everywhere you look, the rivers' steady flow the result of a bountiful winter. As tempting as it might be to get on the trails as soon as summer starts, oftentimes you cannot hike certain trails until mid-July or even later than that. The high peaks of the Zirkels and areas in the Flat Top Mountains can and do hold snow in pockets year-round. Many of the shaded trails near town can be muddy later than you think as well. I have noted which of the trails tend to thaw out a little earlier, but it is also important to check conditions of the roads and trails when planning your hike by first by calling the US Forest Service at (970) 870-2299.

The summer of 2016 was a challenging one with regard to fires, the smoke from said fires, and the resulting trail closures. As of this writing, the Beaver Creek fire had burned more than 38,000 acres of wilderness, though impending snow put an end to that. Thick plumes of smoke could be seen from town and surrounding valleys all summer long; some days the smoke would blow into town and linger for a bit until the winds would change course, providing relief.

The Flat Tops from Mandall Lake Trail.

There was also a wildfire up Lynx Pass in the Sarvis Creek Wilderness, resulting in the upper portion of Sarvis Creek Trail closing for a period; the smoke is somewhat visible on the cover of this book, in the upper left-hand corner. And the Lost Solar fire, in a remote section of the Flat Tops, gave me a day to remember. I recall my first attempt at hiking the Mandall Creek Trail on a beautiful sunny September day, when, about 3.0 miles in, the winds kicked up, coming from the southeast. I was inundated with thick smoke in a matter of an hour or so even though the fire was many miles away. I turned around, knowing I would have to complete the hike on another day. Yet, on the return, I was rewarded with pink and golden light all around, intense colors reflected off the mountains and aspen trees with leaves already changing; it was a surreal experience of colors and contrasts that I won't soon forget.

The hardest part of this book was narrowing the trails down to 20. If you are like me, the best trail to hike is the one I'm on today. Rather than making a finite statement that these are the absolute best, I like to think of this book as showcasing twenty of the best trails that aren't too far away from the town center, including varying degrees of difficulty and mileage, so that there is something for every-one- from the seasoned hiker to the new family with kids in tow. I have noted where there are options to hike farther, if you so choose. I hope this book gives you a taste of what Steamboat has to offer, and I also encourage you to explore beyond what is listed here.

—*Jacquelyne Cox*

Indian paintbrush.

The Ten Essentials

1. **Hydration.** Carry at least a water bottle on any hike. For longer hikes, carry more. Keep an extra water container in your vehicle and hydrate both before and after your hike. A pack with a built-in hydration system makes it even easier to stay hydrated while you are hiking. Don't wait until you are thirsty—drink often.

2. **Nutrition.** Eat a good breakfast before your hike; pack a full and healthy lunch, including fruits, vegetables, and carbohydrates. Carry healthy snacks such as trail mix and nutrition bars.

3. **Sun Protection.** Use a broad-spectrum sunblock with an SPF rating of 30, and reapply often. Wear sunglasses and a wide-brimmed hat. Also use lip balm with an SPF rating. These protections are important anywhere in Colorado, especially at high elevations and in desert areas. Bug repellant is especially helpful and necessary in spring and summer months and any place near water.

4. **Insulation.** Be aware that weather in Colorado can go through extreme changes in a very short time. Think warm and think dry—even in arid areas. Dress with wool or synthetic inner and outer layers. Cotton retains moisture and does not insulate well; it should never be part of your hiking gear. Carry a warm hat, gloves, extra socks, and a packable insulating layer such as a down puffy. Always include a waterproof rain jacket and pants—on you or in your pack. Extra clothing weighs little and is a great safety component.

5. **Navigation.** You should attain at least minimal proficiency with a map and a good compass. A GPS unit or GPS app on your smartphone can add to your ability, but it's not a substitute for the tried and true map and compass. Before a hike,

study your route, and the surrounding country, on a good map of the area. Refer to the map as needed on the trail.

6. **Illumination.** Include a headlamp or flashlight in your gear with fresh batteries. With a headlamp, your hands are kept free. Avoid hiking in the dark if at all possible.

7. **First Aid.** Buy or assemble an adequate first-aid kit.

   Some items to include:
   - Gauze and bandages; a bandana, which can double as a sling
   - Duct tape—good for a bandage, blister protection, or rips in your clothes; moleskin is best for blister protection.
   - Alcohol wipes for cleaning a wound
   - Latex gloves
   - Medications for bug bites, allergies, and/or pain

   Note: this is not a comprehensive list—tailor it and add items for your own perceived needs and intended activities.

8. **Fire.** Avoid open fires except in emergency situations. For when you may need to build a fire, carry waterproof matches in a watertight container, a lighter, or a commercial fire starter such as a fire ribbon. Keep these items dry and ensure that all of them will work in cold or wet weather. If needed, tree sap or dry pine needles can help start a fire.

9. **Repair Kit and emergency tools.** A pocketknife or multi-tool and duct tape or electrician's tape are good for various repairs. A SPOT GPS Satellite Messenger allows you to reach emergency responders and share your coordinates at the push of a button in an emergency. It also allows for family or friends to track your whereabouts, especially helpful when hiking in remote country. It's an invaluable tool using modern technology. But even then, sometimes the thickest woods can block a signal, and batteries do die. That's why

carrying a signal mirror and a whistle are still the best bet for when you need to be located in an emergency.

10. **Emergency Shelter.** Carry a space blanket and nylon cord or a bivouac sack. Large plastic leaf bags are handy for temporary rain gear, pack covers, or survival shelters. On your way out, use this for trash left by careless hikers.

Wildlife Viewing Tips

Fade into the woodwork (or woods): Wear natural colors and unscented lotions, if any. Be as quiet as possible—walk softly, move slowly.

Keep to the sidelines: Watch animals from a distance they consider safe. Use binoculars or a telephoto lens to get a closer view. Stay away from nests. Use special caution when near moose. They are unpredictable and can charge at you if they feel threatened.

Use your senses
- **Eyes:** Look up, down, and all around for animal or bird signs such as scat, nests, or tracks. Learn to distinguish these wildlife signatures.
- **Ears:** Listen for animal sounds or movement.
- **Nose:** Be alert to musky scents or strange odors.

Think like an animal: When will an animal eat, nap, drink, bathe?

Optimize your watching: The ultimate wildlife-watching experience is of behaviors—viewing animals without interrupting their normal activities. As a rule, dusk and dawn are the best times for this rewarding experience.

1. Hahns Peak

RATING	Moderate
ROUND-TRIP DISTANCE	3.6 miles
ELEVATION GAIN	1580 feet
ROUND-TRIP TIME	3 hours
MAPS	Trails Illustrated #116 Hahns Peak/Steamboat Lake
NEAREST LANDMARK	Hahns Peak Lake

COMMENT: If you've been to the Yampa Valley, you've probably seen Hahns Peak towering to the north. Its bald, white summit is hard to miss, and the conical shape leaves no guesses as to which peak it is. Situated just northeast of Steamboat Lake and north of rustic Hahns Peak Village (northwest Colorado's oldest settlement), Hahns Peak is a must-do hike. Not only is this landmark mountain steeped in cultural and historical significance for Routt County—prospector mines, remnants, and a fire lookout tower still remain—but also the views from the top are endless. The Lookout Tower, originally constructed in the early 1900s as one of the first fire lookout stations in the Rocky Mountains, was restored at the time of this writing.

Be prepared for thunderstorms and watch the weather closely because this is not a place to be caught in one. Plan ahead, and hike on a day when the weather risk is lowest or nonexistent. Dogs are allowed on this trail, but be forewarned because the volcanic rock and scree near and at the summit can do some damage to sensitive paws. Bring plenty of water because there is no source for humans or canines. Although the trail is short, it is fairly exposed after you hike above tree line. It is not uncommon to read of parties that get lost

The summit of Hahns Peak and the lookout tower as seen from the route.

or disoriented, so make sure you have a map and the proper essentials for hiking up this seemingly innocuous peak.

GETTING THERE: From Steamboat Springs, take US Highway 40 west to County Road 129 (Elk River Road) on the west side of town. Turn right (north) and drive 29.0 miles or so, past Steamboat Lake and historic Hahns Peak Village. After you reach the small town of Columbine, using the general store as a point of reference, look for FR 490 on the right and turn right here. It's easy to drive right past this point, so be sure to slow down after you see the sign for Columbine and the little store. The road from here is rocky and steep and, though passable, a high-clearance vehicle is recommended. At about 0.9 mile, you will come to a junction with FR 410 going off to the right; it is important to stay left here and go up FR 490 another 0.5 mile. It is not uncommon to see cars

Approaching the summit.

The author's dog, Üllr, near the summit.

parked along this stretch, but if your car is able, continue a bit farther up to the designated parking area. Turn left on FR 418, and you will see the parking area in 500 feet.

THE ROUTE: From the trailhead, begin hiking up FR 418. Hahns Peak views are intermittent through aspen groves in this section as well as views looking west toward Nipple Peak. At approximately 0.5 mile, you will see the sign for hiking trail #1158; turn right here and begin the ascent through spruce and fir. At about 1.0 mile you will reach tree line, and the view of the summit and its infamous Lookout Tower becomes more defined. At 1.5 miles you will pass remnants of a mine on your right. Continue upward; from here the trail becomes very steep and rocky. Look for rock cairns to help guide you to the summit. The last stretch is a cinch; the Lookout Tower beckons you to take shelter from wind and provides shade for a nice lunch. Take in the 360-degree views with Wyoming to the north, the Zirkels to the east, and Steamboat Lake and Elk Mountain (Sleeping Giant) and Steamboat Springs to the south. Return the way you came and enjoy the views as you descend.

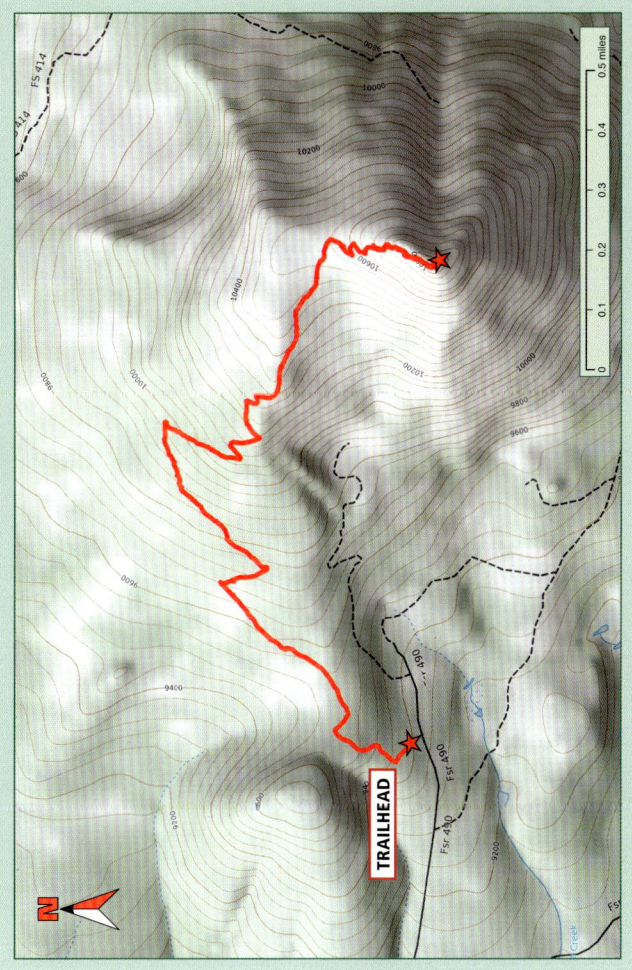

2. Mica Basin

RATING	Moderate–difficult
ROUND-TRIP DISTANCE	8.4 miles (from Slavonia trailhead)
ELEVATION GAIN	2000 feet
ROUND-TRIP TIME	5–6 hours
MAPS	Trails Illustrated #116 Hahns Peak/Steamboat Lake, #117 Clark/Buffalo Pass
NEAREST LANDMARK	Town of Clark

COMMENT: This is one of my favorite hikes in the Zirkels because of its interesting terrain, stunning backdrops, and varied geology. As with much of the Mount Zirkel Wilderness, a severe blowdown ravaged the trees around this landscape in 1997, resulting in a large pine beetle infestation that killed off many of the remaining trees that survived the initial blowdown. And then, in 2002 and 2003, large wildfires swept through the region, the scars they left still evident throughout the Zirkels. Today, this once scarred and scorched zone offers distinct beauty, with a lovely lake at the end of the cirque that includes Big Agnes and Little Agnes Mountains. The lake is home to native Colorado cutthroat trout, a rare find in this state.

The hike is somewhat challenging; after you leave the connecting trail and begin the ascent up the basin, it can be fairly steep and strenuous at times. There are also a few sections of the trail that can be quite muddy. Take care not to hike during the rainy season because this could cause further damage to the trail. Your best bet would be in the later summer months, after runoff, when the trails have had some time to dry out. Though many sites and maps list the round-trip

Little Agnes as seen from Mica Lake.

mileage at 5.0 miles, you must also hike an additional 3.0 miles (1.5 miles each way) of connecting trail to get to the turnoff for the Mica Basin Trail.

GETTING THERE: Directions to the Mica Basin Trail are the same as listed for Gold Creek Lake and Gilpin Lake Trails, ending at the Slavonia Trailhead. From downtown Steamboat Springs, take US Highway 40 west to County Road 129

(Elk River Road) on the west side of town. Turn right (north) and drive to the town of Clark, about 18.0 miles or so. Continue just past the Clark Store and Glen Eden Resort toward Seedhouse Road/County Road 64/FR 400. Turn right. (The turnoff for this road is easy to drive past because it's around a slight curve in the road, so be on the lookout.) Drive 11.0 miles up Seedhouse Road; the road will end at the Slavonia Trailhead. Park here. Because of the popularity of this trailhead (there are other trails accessible from this area), it is best to arrive very early to ensure a parking spot.

THE ROUTE: Beginning at the Slavonia Trailhead, hike 0.25 mile up to the trail junction and trail registers for Gilpin Lake (#1161) and Gold Creek Lake (#1150). Stay left, continuing up the Gilpin Lake Trail. At 1.5 miles, shortly after crossing the Mount Zirkel Wilderness boundary, you will see the sign

The trail ascends towards Mica Lake.

Fireweed and a charred snag along the route.

Big Agnes looms over Mica Lake.

and turnoff for Mica Basin Trail (#1162). Turn left (north) here. This is where the trail begins its steep ascent into Mica Basin, and it doesn't waste any time in doing so. Hike the rocky switchbacks, and before too long you will hear the sounds of Mica Creek off to the east. At mile 2.4 there is a nice waterfall that comes into view amid scars from wildfires that raged more than a decade ago. Just a little farther up, above a few more switchbacks, you finally reach the saddle and first view of Big Agnes and Mica Basin. After a few minutes more you come to a creek crossing. There is no bridge or easier way around it, so plan on getting your feet wet. Shortly after the creek crossing the trail meanders in and out of willows. This section of the trail, as well as a few other spots, can be very muddy, so please tread lightly if hiking during or after a rainstorm.

There are certain sections of this trail where lifeless, leafless trees still stand, providing a glimpse into what the ter-

Wildflowers are abundant along this trail during the summer months.

rain might have looked like before the beetles, blowdown, and burn changed the landscape forever. It's a haunting yet eerily beautiful reminder that nature, though harsh, does recover. The basin floor is thick with wildflowers and greenery during the summer months. One such flower, Chamerion angustifolium, otherwise known as fireweed, thrives in areas cleared by fire. You will see a lot of them in this basin, the pink flowers providing a nice contrast against many of the blackened snags.

At around 4.0 miles you reach another meadow with lovely views all around. Hike another 0.5 mile, and Mica Lake now comes into view. At about 4.2 miles from the start of Slavonia Trailhead, you have reached the shore. Hiking around the lake will easily add another mile to your hike, more if you choose to hike up to the saddle between Big Agnes and Little Agnes. Enjoy the views and then retrace your steps back down the way you came.

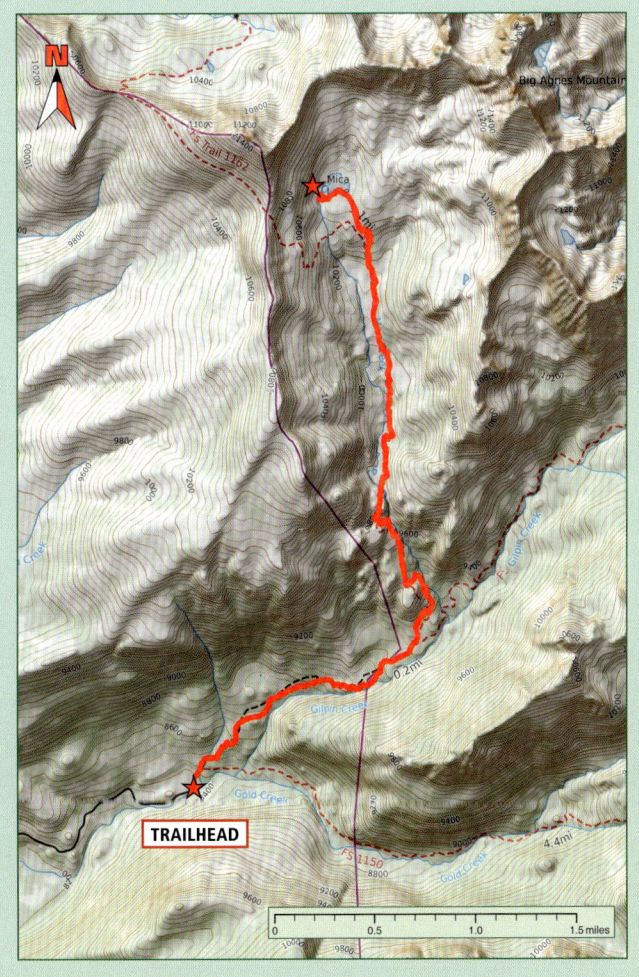

MICA BASIN

3. Gold Creek Lake/ Zirkel Circle

RATING	Moderate
ROUND-TRIP DISTANCE	6.8 miles
ELEVATION GAIN	1,160 feet to Gold Lake
ROUND-TRIP TIME	3–4 hours - Gold Lake
MAPS	Trails Illustrated #116 Hahns Peak/Steamboat Lake, #117 Clark/Buffalo Pass
NEAREST LANDMARK	Town of Clark

COMMENT: Gold Creek Lake Trail is one of the most popular trails located in the Mount Zirkel Wilderness because of its ease of access and shortness if doing an out-and-back. It is rather steep initially as it meanders up and across Gold Creek, and it does require a pretty significant creek crossing (there is no bridge and the log might or might not be there to assist you). Because of this, it is better to hike later in the summer season because the runoff won't be as deep or turbulent. That being said, even in mid-August the water was still up to my shins when crossing, so be prepared. There is a beautiful section of waterfalls visible right off the trail, and the summer months will reward the eyes with a plethora of flowers such as Indian Paintbrush, Columbine, and bright pink fireweed. This trail can be linked with the awesome Gilpin Lake Trail to complete an 11-mile loop otherwise known as the Zirkel Circle—see the note near the end of this section, An Extended Route, on how to hike these trails together.

GETTING THERE: From downtown Steamboat Springs, take US Highway 40 west to County Road 129 (Elk River Road) on the

Gold Creek Lake.

west side of town. Turn right (north) and drive to the town of Clark, about 18.0 miles or so. Continue just past the Clark Store and Glen Eden Resort toward Seedhouse Road/County Road 64/FR 400. Turn right. (The turnoff for this road is easy to drive past because it's around a slight curve in the road, so be on the lookout.) Drive 11.0 miles up Seedhouse Road; the road will end at the Slavonia Trailhead. Park here. Because of the popularity of this trailhead (there are other trails accessible from this area), it is best to arrive very early to ensure a parking spot. This trail does see very heavy use and is best hiked in the fall after the summer crowds have come and gone.

THE ROUTE: The initial section of this trail is #1161—the trail that leads to Gilpin Lake—but the sign at the trailhead is clearly marked. Hike through a mixed forest of pine and aspen for 0.25 mile until you get to the fork for #1150, the Gold

Creek Lake Trail. Be sure to bear right at this point. Before too long you will hear the sound of rushing water. Cross the small footbridge over Gilpin Creek. You will notice the burn area up on the ridge to your right and a nice viewing area at 0.7 mile.

At 1.14 miles you will see the sign marking the Mount Zirkel Wilderness Boundary, and at about 1.7 miles there is a nice, flat rock outcropping giving you a front-and-center view of the waterfalls. I found this a great place for a quick snack and photo opportunity. At this point the trail meanders right next to Gold Creek, and one section of the trail is literally right next to the water; use caution in the earlier months of runoff. At 2.0 miles you will see another trail sign reminding you that you are on the right trail. The creek crossing is here as well. At the time of this writing there was a narrow log to cross, but many like me will opt to cross in the water rather than testing my balance on the log, which sits rather high off the water.

It is important that after you cross the creek, you turn right, because there is a spur trail to the left that looks deceiving. It in fact goes nowhere. So, be sure to turn right after the creek crossing to stay on the main trail. At 2.4 miles you will come across another, smaller creek crossing. I was able to rock-hop with success, but remember, if you are hiking in the earlier summer months, be prepared for heavier runoff and possibly getting your feet wet. From here the trail begins a series of switchbacks as it meanders away from the creek; one section even includes a three-foot high manmade rock wall, presumably to maintain the trail during runoff season. Be sure to look back and admire the view as it only gets bigger from here on out.

The last 0.25 mile of the trail levels out, and finally, at 3.4 miles, you have arrived at the lake. There are some fantastic picnic spots dotted around the lake; find one you like and enjoy the scenery before retracing your steps back down through Gold Gorge and back to the parking area. For those who are looking to hike the Zirkel Circle, read on.

EXTENDED ROUTE: At this point, you have reached Gold Lake. If you have the energy and resources to hike an additional 8.0 miles, or if you are backpacking, you can link this trail up with Gilpin Lake Trail #1161, hiking up and over Circle Pass and then down to Gilpin Lake, alongside Gilpin Creek, and then back to the parking lot, for a total loop hike of 11.0 miles. Continue on the Gold Lake Trail #1150 for 0.5 mile. You will reach a trail junction, with #1150 on your left and the Wyoming Trail (#1101) going to your right. Continue left on #1150. After a brief downhill section, you will encounter another creek crossing with no bridge or logs to assist you. This section is beautiful, with large meadows and the Park Range and Continental Divide skirting to the east.

A waterfall along Gold Creek.

At 1.3 miles after the last creek crossing, you will reach another trail sign and junction; turn left because this is the start of the Gilpin Lake Trail #1161. The next mile or so of hiking is really exhilarating as you climb up numerous switchbacks, exit tree line, and approach the rocky and exposed Circle Pass. At 10,800 feet, the blue-hued Gilpin Lake comes into sight, with stunning views of Big Agnes, the false summits of Mount Zirkel and the Sawtooth Range and Park Range in the background, making for one dramatic alpine scene.

From the base of Gilpin Lake, you have just over 4.0 more miles of easy downhill hiking to get back to the Slavonia

A large meadow and views of the Park Range.

Trailhead, which completes the Zirkel Circle. For more information on the Gilpin side, please read the description on the Gilpin Lake Trail #1161.

NOTE: Though a few Steamboat natives might disagree, I prefer to hike the Zirkel Circle in a counterclockwise fashion (as opposed to clockwise), from Gold Lake up and over to Gilpin Lake, as described here. Although the ascent to Gilpin Lake is mellower than the ascent to Gold Lake and up the pass, the trail is longer getting there, and you still have to hike another 0.5 mile UP to the pass to get the amazing views. To me, these dramatic views provide a sense of wonderment and awe because the view of Gilpin Lake comes as a surprise after you crest the pass coming from the Gold Lake side, and you get to stare in amazement (as opposed to looking behind you) as you descend down toward the lake. I also find merit in knowing the rest of the trail is downhill from here; the hardest part—the uphill climbing—is now behind you.

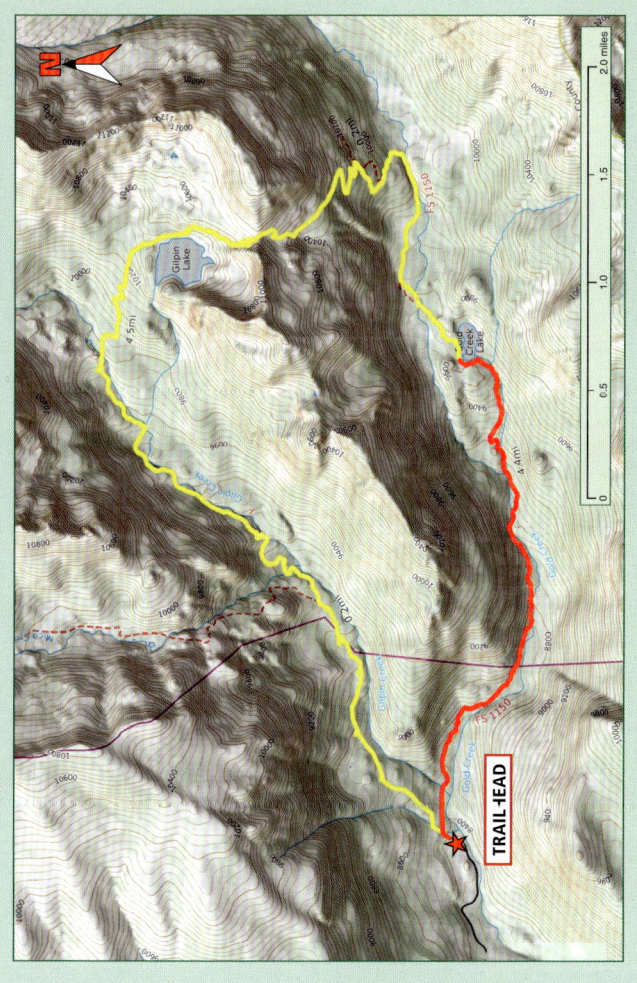

GOLD CREEK LAKE/ZIRKEL CIRCLE

4. Gilpin Lake

RATING	Moderate
ROUND-TRIP DISTANCE	8.0 miles
ELEVATION GAIN	1900 feet to Gilpin Lake
ROUND-TRIP TIME	6–7 hours
MAPS	Trails Illustrated #116 Hahns Peak/Steamboat Lake, #117 Clark/Buffalo Pass
NEAREST LANDMARK	Town of Clark

COMMENT: This is probably the most popular hike in Routt County, judging by the number of people hiking on the trail on any given weekend, especially in the summer. It's practically impossible to have this trail all by yourself, though I found hiking this on a weekday to be much less crowded than on the weekends. The lake is nestled below Mount Zirkel, and the backdrop of this mountain and others surrounding the lake provide the most picturesque of alpine settings. Gilpin Lake itself has a gorgeous blue hue on most days, and there are numerous spots to photograph and just "take it all in." For hardy or ambitious hikers, this trail can be linked with the Gold Creek Lake Trail to complete the awesome Zirkel Circle. Please note there is no camping within 0.25 mile of the lake, and this is strictly enforced. The trail is well maintained and follows Gilpin Creek most of the way up. As with other trails in this book, be prepared for inclement weather.

GETTING THERE: From downtown Steamboat Springs, take US Highway 40 west to County Road 129 (Elk River Road) on the west side of town. Turn right (north) and drive to the town of Clark, about 18.0 miles or so. Continue just past the Clark Store and Glen Eden Resort toward Seedhouse Road/County

Gilpin Lake.

Road 64/FR 400. Turn right. (The turnoff for this road is easy to drive past because it's around a slight curve in the road, so be on the lookout.) Drive 11.0 miles up Seedhouse Road; the road will end at the Slavonia Trailhead. Park here. Because of the popularity of this trail (as well as Gold Creek Lake Trail, accessible from this area), it is best to arrive very early to ensure a parking spot.

THE ROUTE: Hike through a mixed forest of wildflower-riddled pine and aspen groves for 0.25 mile until you get to the fork for #1150, the Gold Creek Lake Trail; there will be a sign. Take the trail to the left, the Gilpin Lake Trail #1161. There is a gorgeous aspen grove, and you will hike through a few meadows as you work your way uphill. At 1.1 miles you will cross into the Mount Zirkel Wilderness, and at 1.5 miles, you will pass

Jagged peaks along the approach. An old uprooted snag along the route.

the trailhead for Mica Basin. Continue straight ahead. The trail continues northeast, and, after a series of switchbacks, the false summit of Mount Zirkel and the surrounding cirque come into view. There are a few creek crossings but by mid-August I was able to rock-hop across these with no problem. The earlier in the season you hike, the more likely you are to get your feet wet.

There are numerous meadows and photo opportunities as you continue your way up. At about 3.0 miles you will cross one more creek; the trail continues to the right as you then begin working your way south, then east, then southeast up the final stretch toward Gilpin Lake. At 3.8 miles you have reached Gilpin Lake. Return the way you came for a total round-trip hike of around 8.0 miles; or, if you wish, you can hike another 0.5 mile or so up to the saddle (Circle Pass) for fantastic views of the lake. This is also the portion of the trail that links back to the Gold Creek Lake Trail #1150 and then circles back down to the Slavonia Trailhead, thus allowing you to complete the Zirkel Circle in a clockwise fashion if you so choose.

GILPIN LAKE

5. Three Island Lake

RATING	Moderate
ROUND-TRIP DISTANCE	6.8 miles
ELEVATION GAIN	1200 feet
ROUND-TRIP TIME	Approximately 4 hours
MAPS	Trails Illustrated #116 Hahns Peak/Steamboat Lake, #117 Clark/Buffalo Pass
NEAREST LANDMARK	Town of Clark

COMMENT: This is a very nice trail with big views on the initial ascent of Mount Ethel, Lost Ranger Peak, and the Dome, situated to the south. The lake is nestled at 9,800 feet in the Mount Zirkel Wilderness and offers good fishing and aesthetic views. At one point this trail was heavily affected by the 1997 blowdown, but evidence is hardly noticeable to the untrained eye just 20 years later. Please note there is no camping within 0.25 mile of the lake, and this is strictly enforced. Some of the trail is south facing and can be very hot in the summer months, as well as buggy. Plan ahead.

GETTING THERE: From downtown Steamboat Springs, take US Highway 40 west to County Road 129 (Elk River Road) on the west side of town. Turn right (north) and drive to the town of Clark, about 18.0 miles or so. Continue just past the Clark Store and Glen Eden Resort toward Seedhouse Road/County Road 64/FR 400. Turn right. (The turnoff for this road is easy to drive past because it's around a slight curve in the road, so be on the lookout.) Drive 9.0 miles up Seedhouse Road and continue just past the Seedhouse Campground, on your right. There will be a big meadow and a junction with Forest Road 443. Turn right (south) here. Continue up the hill and around

Three Island Lake.

FR 443 for approximately 3.0 miles; the road will eventually head east. The trail begins on the north side of the road—look for the large trail sign so you know you are in the right area. Trailhead parking is minimal; there are just a few spots on either side of the road but no real designated parking.

THE ROUTE: The trail begins with a moderate climb up a few switchbacks for 0.25 mile. At this point, you will find a sign and spur trail off to the left indicating 1163.1a; this is the initial spur trail, which goes all the way back down to FR 443 and links back to Seedhouse Campground. Turn right (east) at this junction to continue up to Three Island Lake. Shortly after turning right, you begin a moderate ascent with few to no trees. Look to the south and you can make out the big peaks in the Park Range, which also straddle a segment of the Continental Divide, the Dome being the most prominent. I hiked this in mid-September, and the fall colors provided an intense and lovely backdrop to this mountain range.

Three Island Creek.

Autumn colors and views looking south.

Eventually you begin to get a little shade relief as the trail winds through a mix of pine and aspen groves. At 0.7 mile the trail begins to get a little steeper before leveling off somewhat. In between miles 1.0 and 2.0 you'll be right next to North Three Island Creek, and at one spot there is a nice area to let Fido get his feet wet. Continue hiking up another series of switchbacks, crossing over into the Mount Zirkel Wilderness Boundary. The last segment of the trail before reaching the lake is nice and flat, crossing through a giant meadow before meandering right next to the creek. At 3.4 miles, you finally reach the lake. Enjoy a picnic lakeside before retracing your steps down the way you came. The trail does continue for another 2.0 miles or so, connecting with the Wyoming Trail #1101, offering a myriad of options of loops and through-hikes for backpackers.

NOTE: If you are camping at Seedhouse Campground, it's possible to begin your hike from there, using the spur trail described at the beginning of this hike. But that spur trail, #1163.1a, is not included in the round-trip mileage listed.

THREE ISLAND LAKE 37

6. Hinman Lake

RATING	Easy
ROUND-TRIP DISTANCE	4.0 miles
ELEVATION GAIN	800 feet
ROUND-TRIP TIME	2 hours
MAPS	Trails Illustrated #116 Hahns Peak/Steamboat Lake, #117 Clark/Buffalo Pass
NEAREST LANDMARK	Town of Clark

COMMENT: This is a great little hike for everyone in the family. It features abundant wildflowers in the spring and summer months, and the highlight is a very pretty receding lake that is home to numerous dragonflies, butterflies, and thousands of yellow water lilies. The trail's southern exposure allows for access earlier in the season than some of the other hikes in the surrounding area. There are no fish in this lake—it's just too shallow—so it is generally less crowded. Those who enjoy botany will really appreciate this hike.

GETTING THERE: From downtown Steamboat Springs, take US Highway 40 west to County Road 129 (Elk River Road) on the west side of town. Turn right (north) and drive to the town of Clark, about 18.0 miles or so. Continue just past the Clark Store and Glen Eden Resort toward Seedhouse Road/County Road 64/FR 400. Turn right. (The turnoff for this road is easy to drive past because it's around a slight curve in the road, so be on the lookout.) Drive 6.0 miles. After the pavement ends, turn left onto FR 430, Hinman Lake Road. There is an obvious dirt parking lot on the right. I prefer to park here and hike up this road about 1.0 mile to the actual #1177 TH. At the time of this writing, this road was blocked off because of

Hinman Lake.

very loose and sandy dirt. If the road isn't blocked off, with four-wheel drive it's possible to drive a little farther up this road, but it is pretty rough; I wouldn't push your luck.

THE ROUTE: The initial hike begins on FR 430. Right away you will notice dead trees among the living spruce and fir, sickened from the pine beetle epidemic of 1999. The road undulates for about 0.7 mile before you reach the bridge at Hinman Creek. You will see the sign for Trail #1177; cross the bridge and continue upward. This initial climb is a bit steep, but the switchbacks help. At about the 1-mile point, you see a gate and another trailhead sign; continue straight ahead. A word to the wise: the plants and wildflowers can be very tall during the growing season; therefore hiking pants or ski socks would help keep scratches and bugs at bay. At about 1.6 miles you come to a sign—Hinman Lake goes to the left; Trail #1177 continues to the right for another 4.5 miles. Go

Cow Lily.

A bumblebee feeding on lupine.

left to get to the lake. At around 1.8 miles, the lake comes into view. The lily pads are the round leafs of the yellow pond lily, also known as cow lily. They float on the surface of the water, and in midsummer this massive colony blooms with a bright yellow flowers, a sight to behold. Enjoy the serenity at this lake and retrace your footsteps for the return.

OPTIONAL ROUTE: If you prefer a longer hike when leaving the lake, turn left at the main trail sign for Trail #1177 and continue another 0.5 mile or so, staying right at the fork (ignoring cutover Trail #1188, which goes to the left). Continue another 0.25 mile up trail #1177 past this fork to a spur trail that goes to the right. Hike this for a few minutes and you will get to a nice overlook that sits high above a scree field with Hahns Peak in the distance. Return to Trail #1177, turning left to descend or turning right to continue hiking farther. This trail, also known as Scott's Run, continues north for another 4.0 miles or so to Diamond Park, popular with mountain bikers and ATVers. You can hike it as far as you'd like before turning around and hiking south, the way you came.

HINMAN LAKE

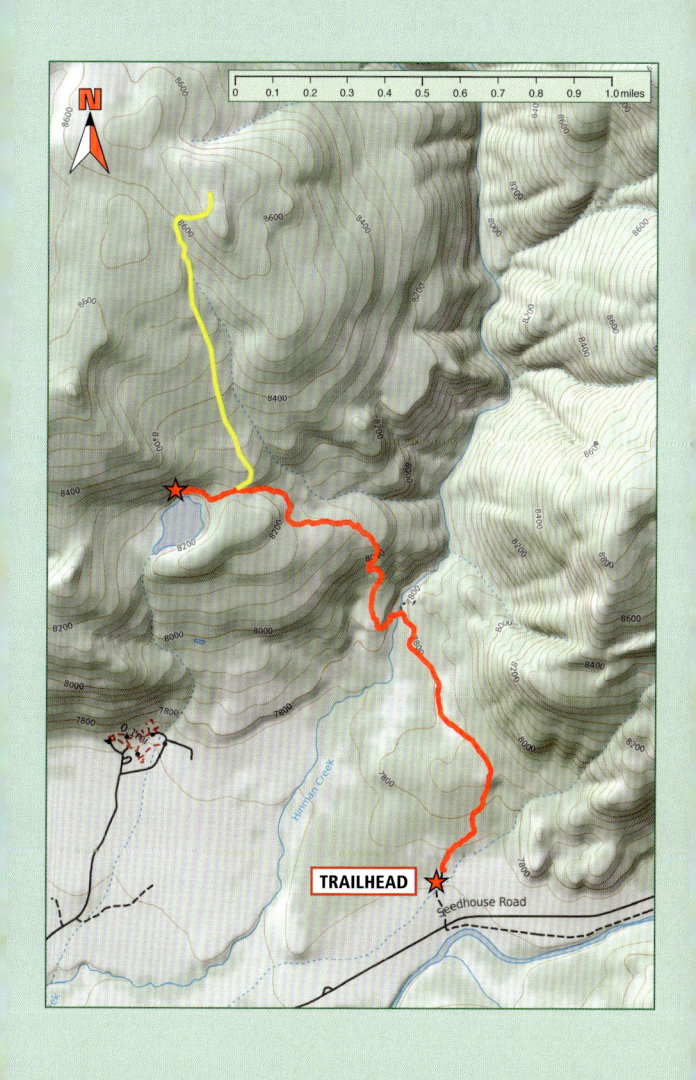

7. Mad Creek and Saddle Trail

RATING	Easy–moderate
ROUND-TRIP DISTANCE	5.6 miles
ELEVATION GAIN	675 feet
ROUND-TRIP TIME	2–3 hours
MAPS	Trails Illustrated #117 Clark/Buffalo Pass
NEAREST LANDMARK	Town of Steamboat Springs

COMMENT: Mad Creek and its sister trailhead to the north, Red Dirt, offer a multitude of routes and loops for hikers and bikers alike. You can add as much mileage as you'd like. And access from town is easy, making this one of Steamboat's most popular networks of trails. Because of these loops and spur trails, many of which are unmarked, it can be very easy to get disoriented and thus find yourself on the wrong trail. To make matters even more confusing, the Mad Creek Trail turns into the Swamp Park Trail past the barn. So even though the trail number stays the same (#1100), the name of the trail changes, depending on which sign you are looking at. Many hikers tend to do an out-and-back from the Mad Creek Trailhead up to the historic 110-year-old Mad Creek barn and then turn around for a total of 4.0 miles, a great hike. I've chosen to include a nice little loop from the Mad Creek barn up through a cutoff trail, then connecting with Saddle Trail #1140, heading south through a nice aspen grove before leading back down near the barn and back to the main trail, then back to the trailhead. Because of the popularity of the trail as well as multiple-user access, dogs should be leashed to avoid any confrontation with bicycles or equestrians' horses.

GETTING THERE: From downtown Steamboat Springs, head west on US Highway 40 and then turn right (north) on County Road 129, otherwise known as Elk River Road. Drive just more than 5.0 miles and then turn right at the Mad Creek Trailhead.

The historic Mad Creek Barn.

THE ROUTE: The Mad Creek Trail is situated on the north side of the Mad Creek Trailhead parking lot. Cross a private driveway and then begin your ascent up a wide trail, heading east at first and then north. The sound of Mad Creek fades in the distance as you work your way farther up the shady canyon. At about 1.3 miles, look behind you—you can see Flat Top Mountain way in the distance. Shortly after, the trail flattens out and the views open up to the north, with Mad Creek barn sitting off in the distance to the left.

At 1.7 miles you will notice spur trails going in both directions off the main trail. Continue straight ahead. At 1.8 miles you come to another spur; go left here; this is the trail that leads up to the barn. It is important not to miss the turnoff for this trail like I originally did. If you seem to be walking past and away from the barn, you probably missed the first cutoff. There will be another spur to your left momentarily; be sure to take a left here and continue up to the barn, passing the first trail to your left that you missed originally. You will see a sign with a nice description and history of the Mad Creek barn. There are also a few rocks where you can have a quick rest and a snack.

From the sign at the barn, to your left there will be a gate with a large rock next to it. Go through this gate and begin hiking on the single track that runs north by north-

THE BEST STEAMBOAT HIKES

Saddle Trail in the fall.

east for about 0.25 mile, up through a large grassy meadow and then through a small stand of aspen. You will come to an unmarked fork; turn left here (east). This is the Saddle Cutoff Trail #1140.1a. Hike up this trail through alder and scrub oak for 0.6 miles, a short distance. The views along this segment looking south are great.

The next fork will be easy to walk past if you are not paying attention, as I almost did, so it helps to know your hiking pace. Take a left at the fork; this is the Saddle Trail #1140. There is a gorgeous aspen stand that you hike through and around for 0.8 mile. You will be headed south as the trail begins to descend before circling back up north, then around northeast, just before heading south again. This segment of trail does not go back to the barn, but instead, as you approach the barn, you will be just south of it. Near the end of this loop you will come to another fork; the barn is also visible from here. If you went left, you would be back up at the barn and the Swamp Park Trail/Mad Creek Trail #1100, but instead stay right at this fork. Go a little farther, cross the gate, and then go right again. You are now back on the Mad Creek/Swamp Park Trail #1100 and headed back to the trailhead.

MAD CREEK AND SADDLE TRAIL 45

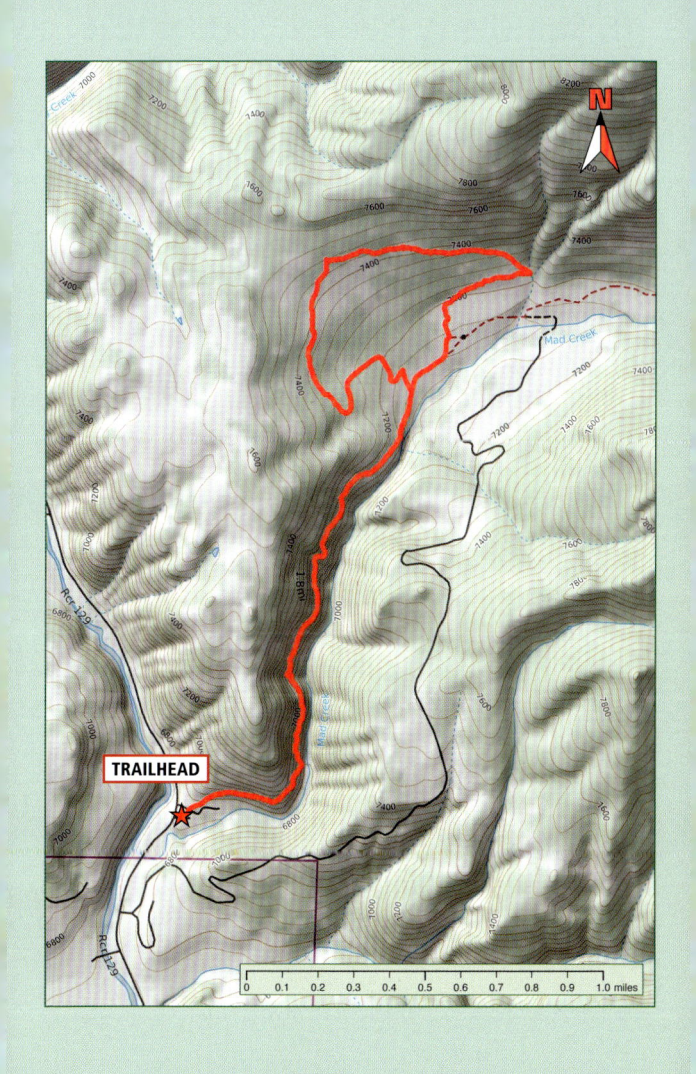

8. Strawberry Park Hot Springs Hike

RATING	Easy
ROUND-TRIP DISTANCE	6.2 miles
ELEVATION GAIN	715 feet
ROUND-TRIP TIME	2–3 hours
MAPS	Trails Illustrated #117 Clark/Buffalo Pass
NEAREST LANDMARK	Town of Steamboat Springs

COMMENT: This is an easily accessed trail just a short drive from town, in lower elevations, that will treat you to a natural hot spring soak at the famous Strawberry Park Hot Springs if you so desire. Bikes are allowed on this trail so you will see a few. Leashed dogs are also allowed on the trail, but they are not allowed at Strawberry Park Hot Springs, so leave them at home if you plan to soak. There is a fee to soak in the hot springs, so you must check in at the main gate after hiking up to gain entrance to the springs themselves.

GETTING THERE: From downtown Steamboat Springs, head west on US Highway 40 and then turn north on County Road 129, otherwise known as Elk River Road. Drive just more than 5.0 miles, and then turn right at the Mad Creek Trailhead. Do not hike the trail at this parking lot, but instead walk back to County Road 129, turn left, and walk south on the side of the road for 400 yards; this path is well used and obvious. Then turn left onto an unmarked farm road. There is a sign for the hot springs trail right under a "No Parking" sign. There are also "Private Property" signs posted at the entrance for the areas on both sides of this road. Stay on this road for 0.5 mile, crossing two gates along the way, and then

Hot Springs Creek runs alongside most of the trail.

you will see a sign at a fork marking the trail to the right. This is the trail to the hot springs.

THE ROUTE: Because this hike is at a lower elevation nearer to town, prepare to be warmer than you would at higher elevations. The nice thing is you can hike this very early on in the season in most cases. The trail starts off with no shade, but after 0.7 mile relief is in sight because it meanders next to Hot Spring Creek for the duration of the hike. At around 2.0 miles on the left side of the trail, look for the tree that provides a

The trail sign for Hot Springs Trail #1169.

large, romantic canopy for cover. Perhaps this could be a good spot to put on your bathing suit.

The lush green ferns along the upper portion of this trail signal that you are getting closer, until you see an actual wooden sign for Strawberry Hot Springs. Climb a few hundred more yards along the shaded trail next to a large rock wall, and then you have arrived. You will see some wooden wagons to your right along the creek, and to your left, the new bathroom structure. You must pay the entrance fee to the hot springs in order to use these facilities, so please be respectful. Return the way you came.

NOTE: At the time of this writing, the cost of day use for the hot springs and bathroom facilities varies from $15 to $20 for adults, depending on the season, and $8 to $10 for children under 18. No children under 18 are allowed after dark. Cash only is accepted; credit cards are not. For more information and guidelines to the Strawberry Park Hot Springs, visit the website at http://www.strawberryhotsprings.com.

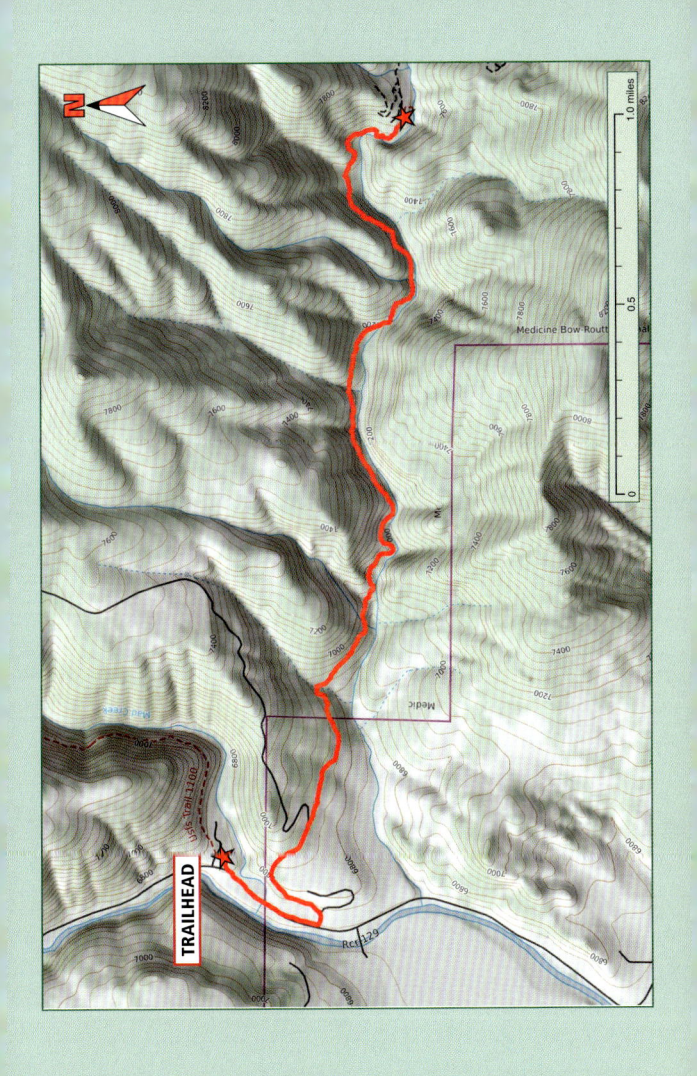

STRAWBERRY PARK HOT SPRINGS HIKE   49

9. Soda Creek

RATING:	Easy
ROUND-TRIP DISTANCE:	3.4 miles
ELEVATION GAIN:	Minimal
ROUND-TRIP TIME:	2 hours
MAPS	Trails Illustrated #117 Clark/Buffalo Pass
NEAREST LANDMARK:	Town of Steamboat Springs

COMMENT: Soda Creek Trail, located up Buffalo Pass Road close to town, is a good hike for all ages, and the trailhead is easily accessible by car. The trail is actually an old US Forest Service road now closed to vehicles. It's also a popular cross country/snowshoe trail in the wintertime. As of this writing, there are approved plans to improve the existing trail and add 30 more miles of trails in the surrounding area for different user groups. This is also a good hike to do if you are camping at the adjacent Dry Lake Campground because no driving is required to access the trail from your campsite. This trail is dog friendly.

GETTING THERE: From Lincoln Avenue in downtown Steamboat Springs, turn north onto Third Street. Go one block and then turn right (at the post office) onto Fish Creek Falls Road. Drive 0.2 mile, and then turn left onto Amethyst Drive. Drive north on Amethyst for 2.5 miles, and then take a right on Buffalo Pass Road (County Road 38). This road starts out paved, but after 1.0 mile or so it turns to dirt, though still passable with two-wheel drive. At 3.0 miles up Buffalo Pass Road, you will see Dry Lake Campground on your left, with a little bit of parking just before the entrance to the camp-

Views along the route in autumn.

ground. Park here. If the lot is full, there is an additional, larger parking lot just across the road on the right.

THE ROUTE: From the small parking lot on the left-hand side of the road, at the entrance to the Dry Lake Campground, begin your hike toward the campground. Walk approximately 275 feet. There will be a closed green gate to your right with a sign stating "Service Road, Closed to Public Use." On that same gate there is a smaller, less obvious sign that says "Trail." Turn right here.

NOTE: At the time of this writing, many improvements and additional trails were in the process of being built. It's quite possible that better signage will exist for this trail in the near future.

The trail begins on what was obviously an old Jeep road, staying just right of the campground. It quickly narrows to mostly single track because time has allowed the ferns and

Soda Creek access from the spur trail.

Fall colors line the route.

bushes to reclaim their fair share of the trail. At around 0.4 mile, you will encounter a spur trail that goes off to the right; stay left here and continue. At 0.66 mile, the trail opens up to views of the surrounding valley. Just a little farther, at 0.8 mile, the trail begins to slope gently downhill, with a small spur trail that goes off to the left. Stay to the right if you wish to continue the main hike, but the spur to the left is worth exploring because it only takes a few minutes, providing a nice shady, sandy spot to access the water. Hike back up this spur and then turn left to get back on the main trail to continue.

From this point on the trail is relatively flat as it meanders just to the south of Soda Creek. At 1.7 miles you'll be at Soda Creek Park, a very large meadow dotted with large boulders. It contains a wooden sign that has long since faded, the information on it lost some time ago to weather, having been buried under feet of snow in the winters over the years. Most people choose to turn around at this spot, but feel free to continue up the faded trail for as long as you like. Retrace your footsteps the way you came.

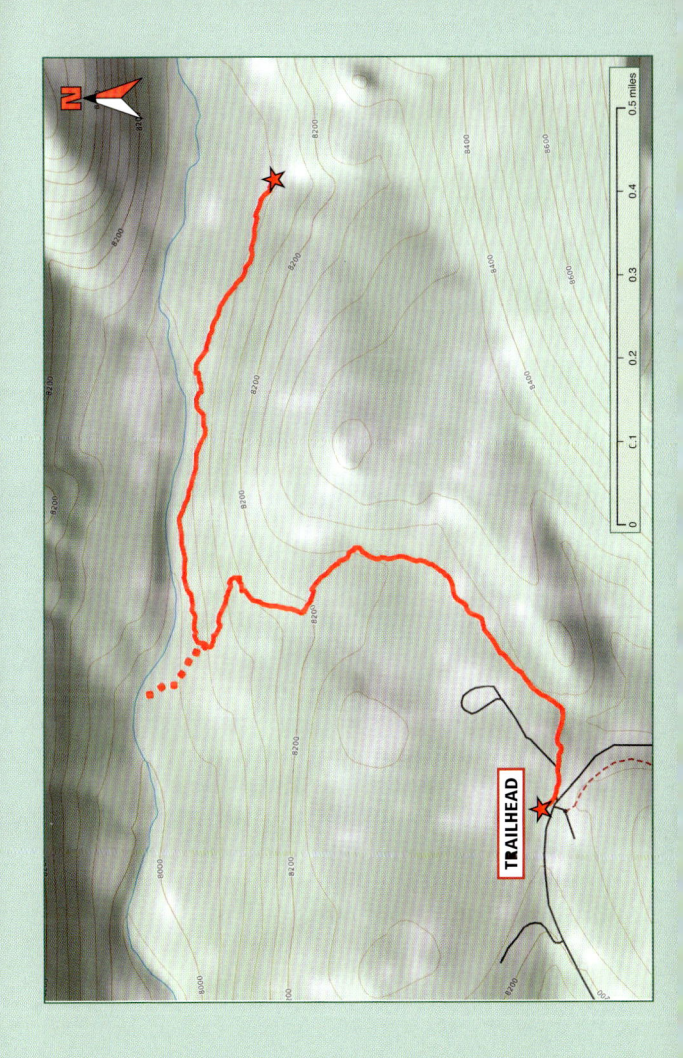

SODA CREEK

53

10. Grizzly Lake

RATING	Easy
ROUND-TRIP DISTANCE	6.0 miles
ELEVATION GAIN	Minimal
ROUND-TRIP TIME	3 hours
MAPS	Trails Illustrated #117 Clark/Buffalo Pass
NEAREST LANDMARK	Buffalo Pass

COMMENT: This wide, short, and easy trail, part of the Continental Divide Trail, is suitable for all ages. It's a short segment of the formidable Wyoming Trail, which runs from the top of Rabbit Ears Pass all the way north past the Wyoming border for a whopping 47 miles. There are lots of little ups and downs, but overall the trail is relatively flat, meandering through pine forests and expansive meadows, offering glimpses of distant peaks as well as Rabbit Ears to the south/southeast. And even though this trail allows ATVs and motorcycles, I saw not a soul when hiking this on a weekday during the first week of August. This trail is very easy to get to if camping at Summit Campground, which is also at the top of Buffalo Pass and is a great option if you have a younger family and want to get the little ones accustomed to the great outdoors. The best months for viewing the wildflowers along this trail are late June through the first part of August.

GETTING THERE: From Lincoln Avenue in downtown Steamboat Springs, turn north onto Third Street. Go one block and then turn right (at the post office) onto Fish Creek Falls Road. Drive 0.2 mile, and then turn left onto Amethyst Drive. Drive north on Amethyst for 2.5 miles, and then take a right

Reflections on Grizzly Lake.

on Buffalo Pass Road (County Road 38). This road starts out paved but after 1.0 mile or so it turns to dirt, still passable with two-wheel drive, though a high-clearance vehicle is best for the last 4.0 miles or so because you must navigate over larger rocks. Drive northeast for about 13.0 miles, going just past Summit Lake Campground on your left. Stay to the right on the road at the junction, driving past the parking lot for Summit Lake. Don't park here, but instead continue south on FR 310 for a few hundred feet; on your left-hand side there will be a designated parking lot for trailers. Park here. The trail climbs up from the southern end of the parking lot.

THE ROUTE: The hardest part of the hike is literally the first few hundred feet because you ascend to a meadow; the trail flattens from here. Very quickly, views of the Zirkels and Summit Lake open up to the north while meadows welcome you with showy displays of daisies and more. If you look away from the amazing views to the north, you can see a com-

Looking north from the start of Grizzly Lake Trail, #1101.

munication tower off to your right and then, a little farther, you will see a power line. Eventually the trail goes under the power line and fades out of view, while Rabbit Ears becomes visible to the south. Stay to the right at the fork in the trail when crossing under this power line, and continue through more meadows.

At one point there used to be a sign here but all that remains now is the sturdy wooden post, the sign long gone. A little farther from here you will see another wooden pole, also with no sign. At about 2.5 miles there will be a very large pond to your left; a spur trail will beckon you to hike to it, but it's important to note that this is not Grizzly Lake! Continue on the trail for another 20 minutes or so; the lake will be visible through the trees on your left. After enjoying the peaceful lake, return the way you came, stopping to admire the flowers all along the way.

GRIZZLY LAKE

11. Emerald Mountain Quarry/Blackmere

RATING	Easy
ROUND-TRIP DISTANCE	3.8 miles
ELEVATION GAIN	872 feet
ROUND-TRIP TIME	1.5–2 hours
MAPS	Trails Illustrated #118 Steamboat Springs/Rabbit Ears Pass
NEAREST LANDMARK	Town of Steamboat Springs

COMMENT: Emerald Mountain sits right in town and offers a multitude of trails for hikers, bikers, and equestrians, mostly single track. It's also home to Howelsen Hill, the oldest operating ski resort in North America. Emerald is truly a special place—some say the jewel of Steamboat. It defines the outdoor lifestyle that draws many people here in the first place, myself included. Blackmere Drive, although a dirt road, offers the most direct way to get to the old sandstone quarry, which offers eye-popping views. It's also the safest bet when ascending the mountain as a hiker, especially with kids, because most of the other trails are used by mountain bikers and can be quite busy, most notably during the weekends. The quarry overlook is a great spot that offers sweeping views of Steamboat Springs, Mount Werner (home of Steamboat Ski Resort), the vast Yampa Valley, and the many mountains that surround it. Bring a camera, sunblock, water, and enjoy. The road is closed to public traffic, though you may see an occasional maintenance truck. Dog owners are required to leash and pick up after their dogs, and this is strictly enforced.

GETTING THERE: From downtown, head west on US Highway 40 (Lincoln Avenue). Turn left (south) on Thirteenth Street, then left on Gilpin Street, left on Saratoga, then right on Routt Street. Park along the right side of the road near the top. The trail begins at the closed gate near the trail sign.

THE ROUTE: Begin your hike up the gravel road right next to a large meadow, one of many on Emerald Mountain. You can see the Sleeping Giant (Elk Mountain) just a little way up to the northwest. Continue up, passing by many of the single-track trails with names such as NPR (No Pedaling Required, a downhill bike-only trail), Emerald Meadows, and MGM. The grade is mellow as it climbs up through scrub oak and then aspen, though there isn't much shade for the entire

Looking east toward Mt. Werner and Steamboat Ski Area at sunset from the quarry overlook.

The hike to the quarry along Blackmere Drive is closed to vehicles and is great for families.

Mule's Ear can be seen along much of the route.

route. Be sure to stay on the main trail because it can get confusing without a map if you end up on a spur trail. The views get better with each step as the trail generally heads in a southerly direction for most of the way. After about 45 minutes of hiking, you see a nice plaque at the overlook as well as numerous rocks to sit on and enjoy the view. You will see many a biker resting here as well. Be careful of the cliffs because they are unstable. Retrace your steps as you take in even more views on the descent.

EMERALD MOUNTAIN QUARRY/BLACKMERE 61

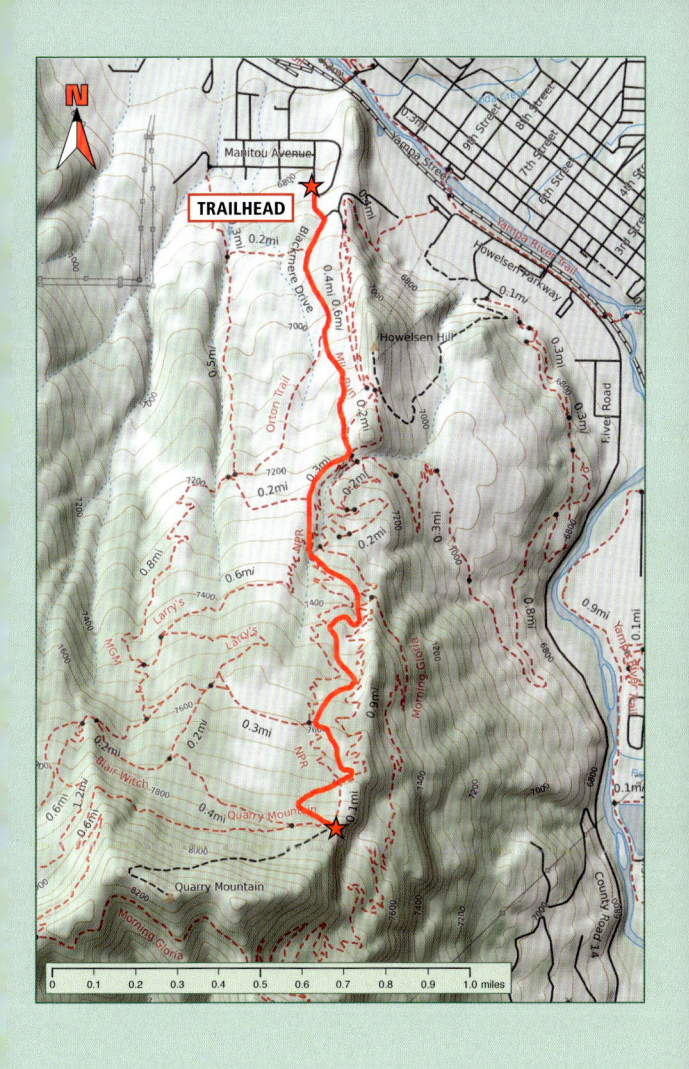

12. Spring Creek

RATING	Moderate
ROUND-TRIP DISTANCE:	10.4 miles
ELEVATION GAIN	1453 feet
ROUND-TRIP TIME	6 hours
MAPS	Trails Illustrated #117 Clark/Buffalo Pass, #118 Steamboat Springs/Rabbit Ears Pass
NEAREST LANDMARK	Town of Steamboat Springs

COMMENT: This hike is truly a gem for all Steamboat residents and visitors alike, open to hikers, bikers, and equestrians. Access to the trailhead is right in town, and the trail offers a great climb up through a gorgeous canyon, home to a vast array of wildlife and plants. My favorite time to hike this is in late August or the first few weeks in September, where the colors of the plants and shrubs and changing aspen are all a feast for the eyes. The trail ends at Buffalo Pass, near the Dry Lake Campground and Soda Creek Trail. There are 15 numbered bridges crisscrossing Spring Creek, a fun way to measure how far you have hiked. Please note that the upper section of the trail is closed from November 15 through April 15 to protect foraging elk, so please respect this closure by not hiking the area during this time frame. There are ponds, a dog park, and a covered picnic area on the lower section of the trail. Dogs are allowed, though they must be on a six-foot leash at all times, and waste must be removed immediately. This is required by law and is strictly enforced, even if you are just walking your dog to the dog park. Hikers must stay to the right on the trail at all times. This is to lessen the chance of any run-ins with mountain bikers descending. Please respect the rules and help keep Spring Creek safe and open to all.

The canyon of Spring Creek Trail boasts early fall colors.

GETTING THERE: From Lincoln Avenue in downtown Steamboat Springs, turn north onto Third Street. Go one block and then turn right (at the post office) onto Fish Creek Falls Road. Drive 0.2 mile, and then turn left onto Amethyst Drive. Drive another 0.3 mile, past the church, and then turn right on East Maple. This is the parking lot and trailhead for Spring Creek.

THE ROUTE. The trail initially starts out as County Road 34; follow this for the first 0.5 mile to the ponds. Stay to the left at the fork after you reach the ponds to continue up Spring Creek because going right takes you to the dog park, bathrooms, and picnic area. You'll cross your first bridge shortly. After crossing the second bridge, just past the 2-mile point, you will see a sign noting that you are entering the Spring Creek Mountain Preserve. This is the upper section of the trail, which is closed November 15 to April 15 every year.

Lush foliage of Spring Creek as summer comes to an end.

Just past this sign, the trail takes an abrupt turn uphill and to the right. Continue upward. The trail from here on out is a nice, smooth single track, riddled with lush ferns in the summertime. It offers more shade as you hike farther up the canyon. The canyon walls display a gorgeous pallet of reds, oranges, and gold if hiked in late summer or early fall; my favorite time to go. At around 3.0 miles there is a steep, rocky section, a rock garden of sorts. A large log here is great for a quick lunch and rest before continuing up. Bridge 11 is just prior to 4.0 miles, with three more of them coming up in quick succession. Bridge 15, the last one, is at just more than 4.5 miles and also right before a large switchback that begins the final push to the top of the trail. There is a slight descent as you approach the end of the trail, near the large parking lot, with Dry Lake Campground across the road. Make use of the shady bench for some rest, and return the way you came, enjoying the subtle beauty this canyon offers.

NOTE: If you have two cars, it's possible to arrange for a shuttle, thus making the hike a one way, either up or down, cutting the mileage in half to 5.2 miles. Park at the large lot across from the Dry Lake Campground on Buffalo Pass; directions on how to get there are listed in the Soda Creek Trail, described in this book.

SPRING CREEK 65

13. Uranium Mine

RATING	Moderate
ROUND-TRIP DISTANCE	3.0 miles
ELEVATION GAIN	800 feet
ROUND-TRIP TIME	2 hours
MAPS	Trails Illustrated #118 Steamboat Springs/Rabbit Ears Pass
NEAREST LANDMARK	Fish Creek Falls

COMMENT: This is a great little hike, accessed via the Fish Creek Falls Trailhead, and is also a popular trail for snowshoeing in the wintertime. At the time of writing, the beginning of the trail is unmarked, and thus it will oftentimes be much less crowded than the Fish Creek Falls hiking trail. It offers a bird's-eye view of the Fish Creek waterfall down below, and also features an abandoned uranium mine at the top of the trail, with an interpretive sign and history of the mine for which this trail is now named. The trail has a bit of a climb at first but then becomes less steep, providing unsurpassed views of Steamboat Springs as well as a glimpse of the ski area.

GETTING THERE: From town, head north on Third Street, then take a right on Oak Street (which turns into Fish Creek Falls Road). Drive 3.0 miles east to the trailhead parking lot. There are two lots, an upper lot and a lower lot. If the upper lot is full, you must park at the lower lot and hike 500 feet or so up on the paved sidewalk. The trail is unmarked and to your left, just past a wooden bench. If you are parked in the upper lot, walk down the paved sidewalk that begins just past the restrooms for about 200 feet. There is a metal drainage grate

A bird's eye view of Fish Creek Falls from the Uranium Mine Trail.

built into the sidewalk; the trail begins to the right just past it. There is a $5 parking fee payable by cash or check. Leashed dogs are allowed.

THE ROUTE: It's hard to believe this was once a road accessed by vehicles servicing the mine because the flowers and bushes have long since filled in the double-track path, making it a narrow trail. The trail begins an immediate climb up a few narrow switchbacks. At about 0.6 mile you get your first glimpse of Fish Creek Falls below. Hike just a bit farther and turn around to see the Yampa Valley and views of the Flat Tops in the distance. At about 0.75 mile up, you will come to a junction with a large rock outcropping, with what appears to be a trail going to the left; stay to the right here because

Looking south towards the Flat Tops from the trail.

Geranium on Uranium.

Veins run through this large rock spotted along the route.

the path to the left is a dead-end. A few hundred feet more and you come across another faint footpath; stay right again and continue up the trail through aspens and ferns.

At about 1.3 miles, you reach the Fair U Uranium Prospect Mine. It is not accessible, but you can see the mine entrance as well as the old rails protruding from the ground, used during the excavation process to transport ore. The trail continues for another 1,600 feet or so past the mine before ending at a spot right next to North Fork Fish Creek. Turn around and return the way you came, remembering to stay left at both forks you see as you make your way back down.

URANIUM MINE

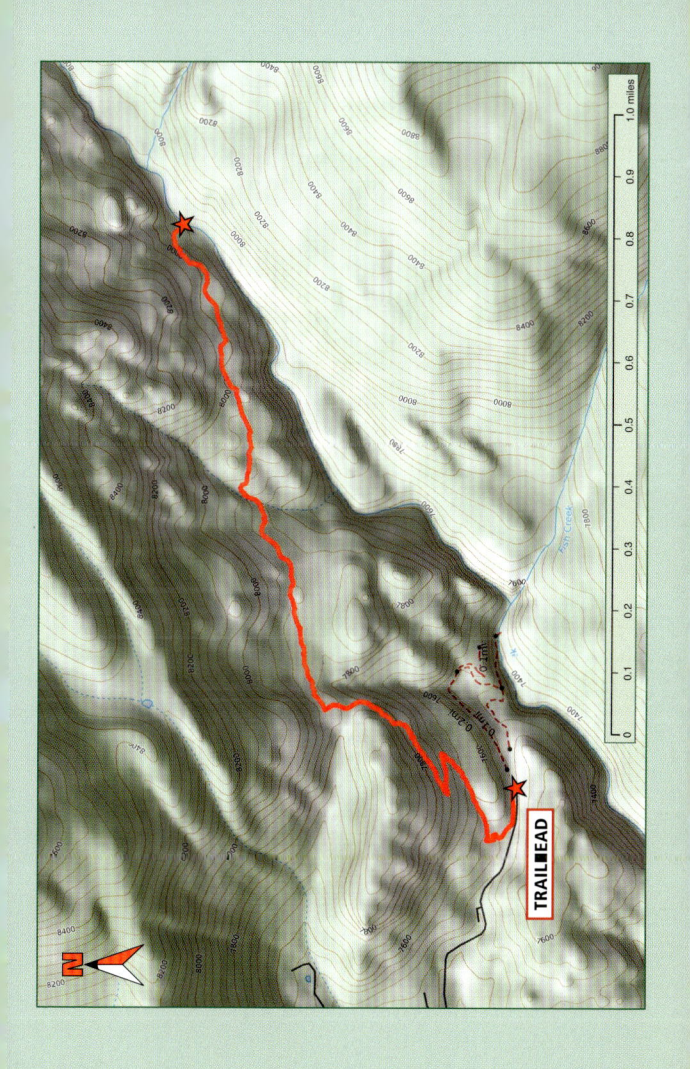

14. Fish Creek Falls/ Upper Fish Creek Falls

RATING	Easy (lower falls); moderate (upper falls)
ROUND-TRIP DISTANCE	0.6 mi (lower falls); 4.4 miles (upper falls)
ELEVATION GAIN	1,516 feet (Upper Fish Creek Falls)
ROUND-TRIP TIME	30 minutes (lower falls); 2–3 hours (upper falls)
MAPS	Trails Illustrated #118 Steamboat Springs/Rabbit Ears Pass
NEAREST LANDMARK	Steamboat Ski Area

COMMENT: This is a great little hike for everyone in the family, easily accessible within town, and offers tremendous views of Fish Creek Falls. The path that leads down to the bridge at the Fish Creek Falls viewing area is wide and smooth. The trail becomes narrow, steep, and rocky if you continue toward Upper Fish Creek Falls. In the 1 hour or so time span hiking to the upper falls, you will see rock formations, cliffs, and geology unique to the area as well as views of Steamboat Springs below. The reward at the end is a smaller waterfall that cascades into pools of water in a beautiful setting, with rocks strewn about perfect for a creek-side picnic. Expect this trail to be very busy on weekends and during the summer months, and remember to always yield to uphill hikers when you are descending. Leashed dogs are allowed. A $5 US Forest Service day-use parking fee is required at the entrance. Even though the hike to Upper Fish Creek Falls is 3.0 miles, it is steep and very rocky. Be sure to wear supportive footwear and bring water.

Fish Creek Falls.

Upper Fish Creek Falls.

GETTING THERE: From town, head north on Third Street, then take a right on Oak Street (which turns into Fish Creek Falls Road). Drive 3.0 miles east to the trailhead parking lot. There are two lots, an upper lot and a lower lot. If the upper lot is full, you must park at the lower lot and hike up 0.25 mile on the paved sidewalk to the upper lot, where the trailhead begins. Get there early to avoid the crowds; before 9 a.m. is best.

THE ROUTE: Begin your hike from the upper parking lot; the sign to the trail is clearly marked. Enjoy the wide and gravelly path down to the waterfall. In about 15 minutes, you will reach the bridge, which is a good place to stop for a photo opportunity. At more than 280 feet in length, Fish Creek Falls is a beautiful waterfall to see no matter the season. If you wish to continue to the Upper Fish Creek Falls, continue right on the trail just past the bridge.

From here the trail gets steep and requires stepping over numerous roots and rocks, so be careful of your foot placement. Although the trail is narrow and well defined, evidence

A squirrel warms itself on the rocks near the upper falls.

Thimbleberry are common during mid-summer.

of switchback cutting can be seen in this section. Be sure to stay on the main path and avoid taking shortcuts as others have done over the years. At just over 1.0 mile, the trail does start to level off in beautiful groves of aspen. In late July and early August, wild berries are plentiful and dispersed among the wildflowers that remain from late spring. At 1.3 miles you begin to see views of the canyon walls, incredible schist and gneiss rock formations dating back some 2 billion years ago.

At about 1.6 miles, you cross another footbridge and continue upward. Shortly thereafter, you begin to see views of the Yampa Valley and Steamboat Springs below, including the Sleeping Giant. At approximately 1.8 miles, the trail becomes a little more exposed as you encounter a very steep section that seems to hug a formidable rock wall. Notice the dark and light color bands in the rocks blending together. After crossing this section, take in the views once again and know you are almost to the upper falls. At 2.1 miles Upper Fish Creek Falls come into view. Be careful with your footing in this area if you choose to go down by the water. Soak in the views and return the way you came, yielding to uphill traffic as you descend.

NOTE: This trail continues up toward Long Lake, a man-made lake, another 3.0 miles past the Upper Fish Creek Falls. This ends up to be an 11-mile round-trip hike not intended for this book.

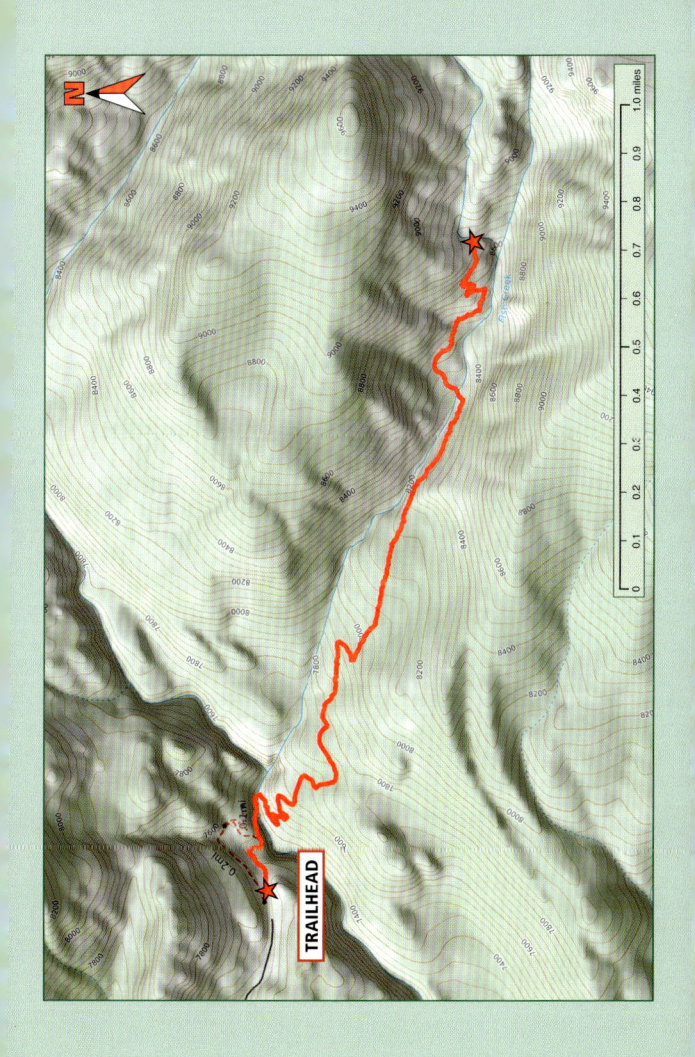

FISH CREEK FALLS/UPPER FISH CREEK FALLS 73

15. Thunderhead Trail

RATING	Moderate
ROUND-TRIP DISTANCE	6.7 miles if hiking both directions
ELEVATION GAIN	2,311 feet
ROUND-TRIP TIME	5–6 hours; less if using the gondola to ascend or descend
MAPS	Trails Illustrated #118 Steamboat Springs/Rabbit Ears Pass
NEAREST LANDMARK	Steamboat Ski Area

COMMENT: It goes without saying that Steamboat Ski Area is known for its abundance of snow in the wintertime. In the summer, the snow gives way to green meadows, aspen and pine groves, and more than 50 miles of trails specific to downhill and free-ride mountain biking, otherwise known as Steamboat Bike Park. Thunderhead Trail, however, is reserved for hikers only. This is an excellent aerobic trail that begins right at the base of the ski area and takes you to the top of the gondola, ending at Thunderhead Lodge. Along the way you are treated to spectacular views of Steamboat Springs as well as the Yampa Valley and the Flat Tops. If you enjoy skiing or snowboarding Steamboat in the winter, this will provide you a new perspective of the mountain while everything is leafy and green. Not to mention that this trail is right in town, easily accessible, and within walking distance if you are staying at any of the resorts nearby. Leashed dogs are allowed.

GETTING THERE: If heading east on US Highway 40 from downtown Steamboat Springs, take the Mount Werner Road exit, then turn left. If headed west on US Highway 40, take the Mount Werner Road exit, then turn right. After you are on Mount Werner Road, look for the Knoll parking lot sign, and park there. Walk down the paved pathway to the left of the parking lot, cross the street, and head toward Gondola Square. Walk directly to the base of the mountain. You will see Burgess Creek and the nice chairs and rocks neatly arranged all around. When you are facing the mountain, the beginning of the Thunderhead trailhead is to the far right. There is a little bridge to cross Burgess Creek, and the official trail begins here. There are signs clearly marking this hiking-only trail.

A sign indicates the start of the Thunderhead Hiking Trail

THE ROUTE: This trail does not waste any time gaining in elevation; hence the moderate rating. Remember, it is a ski resort; you will encounter some steepness when hiking this uphill. The first section of the trail is wide, more like a road, and meanders right next to a downhill-only mountain bike trail to the left and condominiums to the right. At the time of this writing, an alpine slide was under construction in this same area. There is no shade relief here from trees, but do not worry—that will come soon. Enjoy watching the bike riders in this short section, and be sure to stay on the Thunderhead Trail.

At about 0.66 mile, you will notice the Christie Peak Express ski lift to your left. Shortly after this, the hiking trail will intersect with a service road. Look ahead for the trail sign and continue upward, making a sharp right away from the road. From here on out the trail remains single track. You will cross a few bike trails with very obvious signs stating their use for bikes only; be sure to look both ways and yield to bikers. The trail takes you up and across many popular ski runs with names such as See Me, Voodoo, and Vogue, the last of which is

Yampa Valley and the Flat Tops, looking south from the trail.

used for night skiing.

At 1.3 miles you cross another service road, continuing up and along more single track. Thankfully, the switchbacks, of which there are many, take some of the sting out of the elevation gain. Hiking in mid-August, you see an abundance of wildflowers and berries. You gain elevation as you crisscross several popular ski runs known for their moguls.

At 2.8 miles the trail finally begins to level out, crossing under the gondola and rewarding you with sweeping views of the Yampa Valley and the Flat Top Mountains to the south. This last section of the trail meanders through beautiful aspen groves before finally reaching the end of the gondola. There is an opportunity here for restrooms, water, and refreshments at Thunderhead Lodge, assuming it is open. Return the way you came.

OPTIONAL: An added bonus to this trail being located on a ski resort is the ability to utilize the gondola if you or anyone in your party opts for a shorter hike. If you purchase a gondola ticket, you may ride the gondola up and then hike the trail down. Others opt to hike up and then ride the gondola down. Either of these options cut the mileage in half to 3.35 miles. As of this writing, no ticket is needed if you wish to ride the gondola down. Remember, though, that the gondola has shorter operating hours and closes early on certain days of the week, so planning ahead is crucial if you wish to ride it up or back down.

THUNDERHEAD TRAIL 77

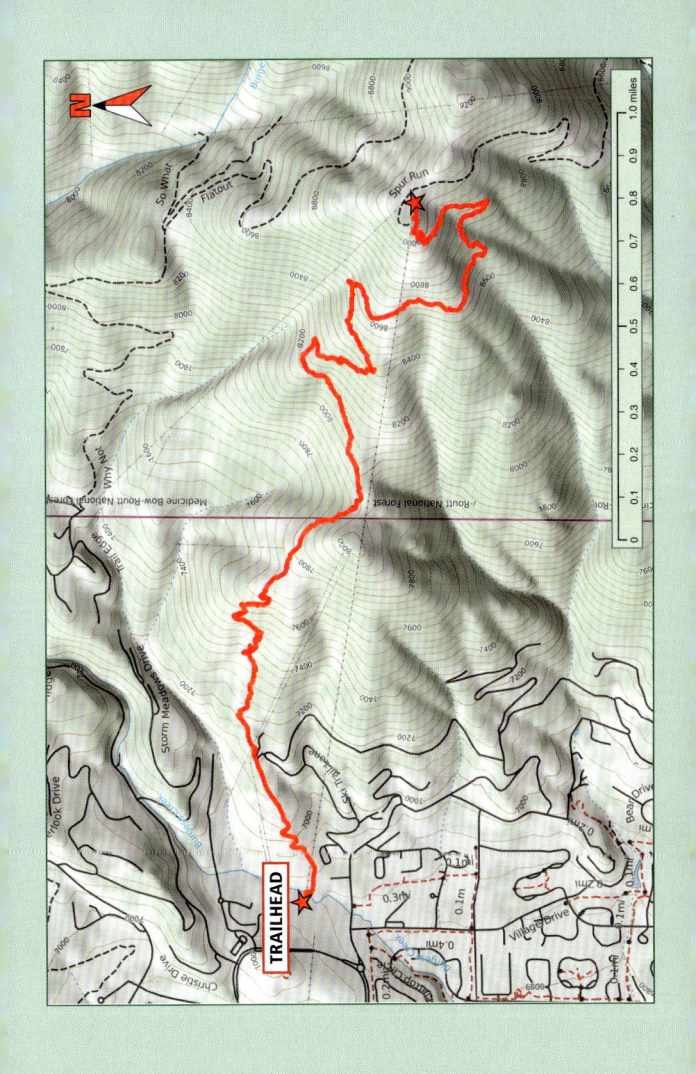

16. Rabbit Ears Peak

RATING	Easy
ROUND-TRIP DISTANCE	6.0 miles
ELEVATION GAIN	1,126 feet
ROUND-TRIP TIME	2–3 hours
MAPS	Trails Illustrated #118 Steamboat Springs/Rabbit Ears Pass
NEAREST LANDMARK	Rabbit Ears Pass

COMMENT: If you've ever driven west toward Steamboat Springs from US Highway 40, then you've more than likely seen Rabbit Ears Peak as you approach Rabbit Ears Pass. They are named aptly for the way the rocks resemble rabbit ears from a distance. Rabbit Ears Peak consists of volcanic breccia—rock fragments cemented together—likely formed after an eruption millions of years ago. These fragments over time have eroded, and as a result, the "ears" are not safe to climb on because of instability. Though time and the elements have ground down these rock formations over the years, the name Rabbit Ears Peak remains.

This is an easy trail, actually an old road, used more by hikers than vehicles, though you will see the occasional ATV or adequately equipped off-road truck. The shortness of this trail, combined with an already high starting elevation at the trailhead, rewards the hiker quickly with amazing views of the Gore Range to the south and the Rabbit Ears Range and Continental Divide to the east. Wildflowers are ample, and the best times for viewing them are June through mid-July. Despite its short distance, the last 0.125 mile of the hike is very steep and strenuous; trekking poles are advised. Bring water, snacks, and plenty of sunscreen and bug repellent.

Views looking south from the trail; haze from the Beaver Creek Fire was visible on this day.

GETTING THERE: From US Highway 40 just east of Rabbit Ears Pass, head north at the turnoff for Dumont Lake and Campground, FSR 315. After approximately 1.0 mile, you'll pass the campground on the left. Continue driving just a bit farther, and turn left at the original monument for Rabbit Ears Pass, erected before the road was rerouted decades ago. Park here, walk up FSR 311 about 0.1 mile, and then turn right (northeast) onto FSR 291, otherwise known as Grizzly Creek Road. Your hike officially begins here. Others choose to drive that short walkable section up FSR 311 and park just after turning right at FSR 291; however, parking is extremely limited here, especially on weekends. It is important to note that if you miss the turnoff for FSR 291, which is easy to do, and instead you continue up FSR 311, you will not be on the right trail.

THE ROUTE: The hike begins at the turnoff for FSR 291, Grizzly Creek Road. Because this is an old road, the trail is nice and wide for families and dogs alike. It is a steady but manageable gain in elevation until the last 0.5 mile, where the trail

Indian Paintbrush with Rabbit Ears Peak in the distance.

A closer view of the ears.

gets very steep. Shortly after your hike begins, the Rabbit Ears formations come into view; there are actually three of them. There are meadows in every direction with stunning views to the south and east. You will cross Grizzly Creek only once on this trail, but I found it easy enough to do a little rock-hopping. Those who wish to hike this trail earlier in the season will more than likely get wet feet at this crossing.

At 1.86 miles, the trail starts to veer more to the east; at the same time it gets considerably steeper before turning south, then southeast, and then north just before reaching the summit of the formations. For the last few hundred feet, the trail is very steep. You can see where the trail has been widened from hikers trying to get traction, stepping off the main trail and further eroding the landscape. Do your best to try to stay on the main trail. Enjoy the views at the Rabbit Ears, but be careful because this is very loose rock; climbing on the formations is not advised. Return the way you came, once again enjoying the tremendous views on the way back down.

RABBIT EARS PEAK 81

17. Sarvis Creek

RATING:	Easy–moderate
ROUND-TRIP DISTANCE:	4.0 miles (bridge); 10.0 miles (cabin)
ELEVATION GAIN:	800 feet (bridge); 1,600 feet (cabin)
ROUND-TRIP TIME:	2 hours (bridge); 5–6 hours (cabin)
MAPS	Trails Illustrated #118 Steamboat Springs/Rabbit Ears Pass
NEAREST LANDMARK:	Stagecoach Reservoir

COMMENT: This is a nice, lesser-traveled trail in the Sarvis Creek Wilderness, just southeast of Steamboat Springs and near Stagecoach Reservoir. Highlights of the Sarvis Creek Trail include a beautiful bridge, lovely picnic spots just over 2.0 miles up, remnants of a logging operation from an era gone by, and an old homesteader's cabin about 5.0 miles up, if your party wishes to hike that far. Numerous brook fishing opportunities abound the higher up you go. Rather than the sweeping alpine vistas that are the hallmark of all other wilderness areas in the state, Sarvis Creek rewards the day hiker with dense forests and meadows, numerous brook crossings, and an amazing array of ferns and wildflowers including Colorado's state flower, the blue columbine. The best opportunities for wildflower observation are late June through mid-July. Dogs are allowed, but they must be leashed or within voice control at all times. Many folks hike 2.0 miles to the very well-maintained bridge and then turn around. However, the trail does continue for another 10.0 miles, up to Buffalo Park Road, so you can hike past the bridge as far as you'd like.

GETTING THERE: From Steamboat Springs, head south on US Highway 40, then right on State Highway 131. Turn left on

Calm waters of upper Sarvis Creek.

County Road 14, also known as Yellow Jacket Pass. Turn left at the entrance to Stagecoach State Park, then immediately bear left at the fork onto County Road 18. Continue on CR 18 over the cattle grate until you come to a fork; make a hard right over another cattle grate into the Sarvis Creek State Wildlife Area and down the hill to access the Sarvis Creek trailhead parking. In years past, you could drive over the bridge and park literally right next to the trailhead, but it appears they keep that bridge gated now except during fall hunting season.

THE ROUTE: From the Sarvis Creek trailhead parking lot, cross the bridge that spans the Stagecoach Reservoir tailwaters. These waters, as well as the numerous secondary creeks that feed into Sarvis Creek, feed into the Yampa River. Tip: the area where you parked is a very popular fly-fishing destination for beginners as well as professional guides; so perhaps bringing your fly-fishing gear along for a post-hike reward is in order. These waters are catch and release only and a fishing license is required.

Head south, then southeast toward the obvious trailhead register, less than 0.25 mile from where you parked. The trail begins with a moderate ascent for 1.5 miles or so before becoming more gradual, with the sounds of Sarvis Creek to your left. This section can be very slick during or immediately after a rainstorm, so be sure you have proper lugged soles for the best traction. There are numerous brook crossings in which dogs can cool off. There is a slight descent and then another ascent before nearing the bridge that crosses

Thimbleberry flowers are abundant in late spring.

Sarvis Creek.

Sarvis Creek. After you cross the bridge at just over 2.0 miles, you will see numerous shady spots along the left side ideal for a picnic. Return the way you came, or continue if you wish to hike up to the old homesteader's cabin.

The trail continues to the right just past the bridge, the elevation becoming more gradual, with Sarvis Creek now nearby and to your right. Interesting rock formations and cliffs dot the landscape. At just under the 3-mile point, a sandy access to the creek is to your right before the trail gives way to a nice view of the creek and numerous fishing holes. Despite the well-defined characteristics of this trail, the luscious ferns and thimbleberry flowers can and will wilt after a rainstorm, thus covering the trail and sweeping across

Cow parsnip.

Columbine are frequently spotted along Sarvis Creek.

your legs at every step. Because of this I recommend hiking in pants or ski socks for added protection. The meadows that meander through the subalpine forests here are a subtle beauty. At about mile 3.2, human-made wooden remnants of the old Sarvis Timber Company, for which this wilderness was named, can be seen along the trail. The company used log flumes to transport wood down to the sawmills.

Continue hiking, and you will see additional remnants of this logging operation here and there as well as numerous wildflowers along the way. At just past the 5-mile point, a large meadow soon gives way to views of an old homesteader's cabin across the creek, down and to the right. From here, explore, have lunch on a rock, and then turn around and begin hiking back the way you came.

SARVIS CREEK 87

18. Devil's Causeway

RATING	Crossing Devil's Causeway is difficult; the rest is moderate
ROUND-TRIP DISTANCE	6.6 miles
ELEVATION GAIN	2,156 feet
ROUND-TRIP TIME	3–4 hours
MAPS	Trails Illustrated #150 Flat Tops North
NEAREST LANDMARK	Stillwater Reservoir

COMMENT: Located in the Flat Tops Wilderness, Devil's Causeway is a must-do hike not just for the Steamboat area but also for the entire state of Colorado. The causeway itself is an arête, or narrow ridge between two cirques—a stretch of volcanic basalt rocks transformed by friction from glaciers melting and receding over millennia. It is only 4 feet wide at its narrowest and 100 feet long, with 1,000-plus-foot drop-offs on either side, passable by hikers only. The views of the surrounding Flat Tops Wilderness Area from the Devil's Causeway are unparalleled. And if you hike it in late June through late July, give yourself extra time to marvel at all the wildflowers along the way. Depending on the previous winter, the upper portion of the trail can be snow-covered and difficult, if not impossible, to hike well into the summer; so check conditions with the Yampa Ranger District before you arrive by calling (970) 638-4516.

GETTING THERE: From Steamboat Springs, drive south on US Highway 40 for just more than 3.5 miles, then turn right (south) on State Highway 131 towards the small town of Yampa. At Yampa, turn right at Main Street; there is a gas station here for reference. Drive through town, and at the

The sweeping view on Devil's Causeway.

end of the road turn left on County Road 7 and continue up the road for about 17.0 miles. CR 7 turns into FSR 900 (Bear River Road) just about where the pavement ends. Along the way you will pass Yamcolo Reservoir, then Upper Stillwater (Yampa) Reservoir, and numerous designated camping sites and campgrounds. At the end of the road, park here. There is a large turnaround as well as pit restrooms. Expect the lot to be full on summer weekends. The trailhead sign is just to the left of the restrooms, next to Stillwater Reservoir (not to be confused with Upper Stillwater Reservoir, which you already drove past).

THE ROUTE: At the reservoir, you will see the trailhead sign for Trails #1119, #1120, and #1122. Access the Devil's Causeway via the East Fork Trail #1119 by staying right as you begin your hike. The first 500 feet or so, you will be swamped with mosquitos and bugs because you are just skirting the lake; I consider this a gauntlet of sorts, not the best way to start your hike, but just know that it ends quickly. I prefer to run this section, as the swarms of mosquitos can be thick. Soon the willows open up to provide views of Stillwater Reservoir, Flat Top Mountain, and Derby Peak.

At 0.7 mile, you will come to a fork with a small sign; continue right (north) on Trail #1119. Very soon afterward, you will cross the Flat Tops Wilderness boundary. Be sure to sign the trailhead register here. Continue climbing up the trail, which now begins its northwesterly ascent up toward the Devil's Causeway. Notice the many downed trees from a previous beetle-kill invasion during the 1930s as you work your way up. At just under 2.0 miles, Little Causeway Lake comes into view. Stay right at the fork because this spur trail goes down to the lake.

Careful footing is required when crossing the causeway.

Looking up towards Devil's Causeway from the trail.

The trail climbs through talus and krummholtz—trees twisted and stunted in their growth—as the elevation continues to increase. Continue up the switchbacks, careful of your foot placement when crossing any patches of snow that remain. Look back down the switchbacks you just hiked, this really is a beautiful trail. At just around 3.0 miles, you are on the saddle. Do not continue on #1119 from here because it is time to head up to the Devil's Causeway. At the time of this writing there is no sign indicating the route. Look for the faint trail that bears left (southwest), and continue up the very steep, but stepped, trail. Use caution in this section and stop when you need to rest; it is quite steep but very doable.

Blue Columbine and Miniature Lupine dot the landscape.

Indian Paintbrush.

After the trail levels off, the Devil's Causeway becomes apparent, the steep slopes on either side of you reminding you of what's next. At this point it is time to commit to cross it, or take a few pictures and be on your merry way back down. When choosing to cross, many people prefer to crawl or crouch down on all fours. Others will walk it as if no big deal. Do use extreme caution, and remember, you must come back the way you came unless you are continuing a loop that will result in a 10-plus-mile hike, not detailed in this book. Do expect to see many other hikers crossing during the weekend and during busy summer months. I prefer to hike this on a weekday, when the chances of seeing others are less, and thus there is no rush when crossing the causeway. Enjoy the hike back down, soaking in the tremendous views of the Flat Tops Wilderness, and revel in the fact that you crossed Devil's Causeway!

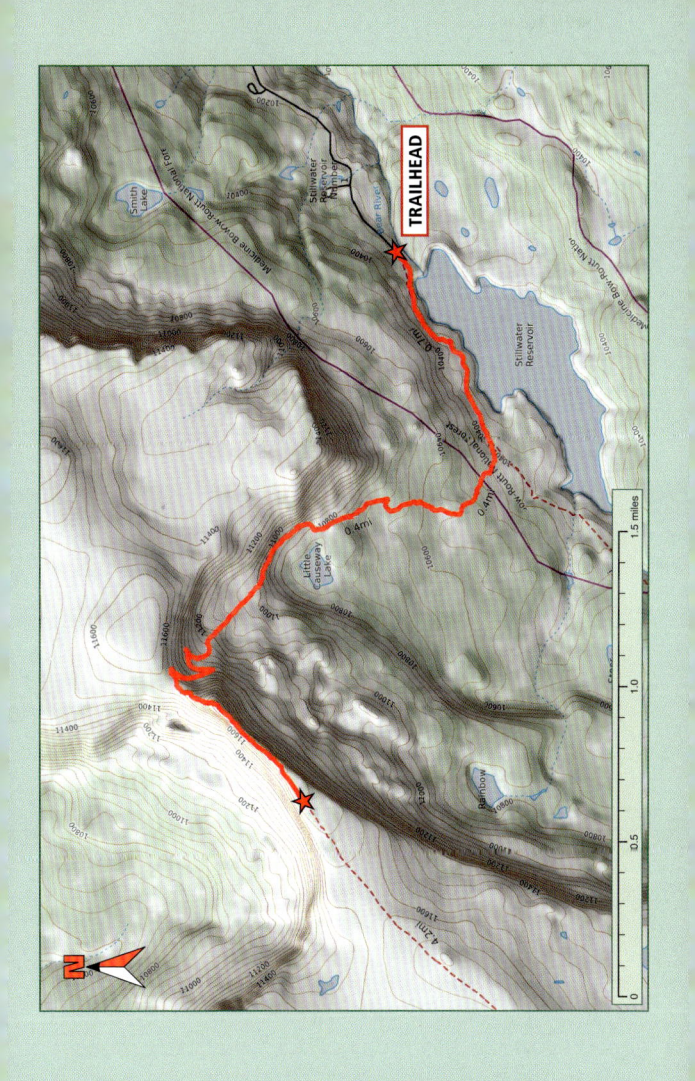

DEVIL'S CAUSEWAY

19. Mandall Lakes Trail/ Mandall Pass

RATING	Moderate to Difficult
ROUND-TRIP DISTANCE	8.0 miles (Black Mandall Lake); 11.0 miles (Mandall Pass)
ELEVATION GAIN	1,300 feet (Black Mandall Lake); 2,000 feet (Mandall Pass)
ROUND-TRIP TIME	4–5 hours (Black Mandall Lake); 6–7 hours (Mandall Pass)
MAPS	Trails Illustrated #150 Flat Tops North
NEAREST LANDMARK:	Town of Yampa

COMMENT: The Flat Top Mountains are very unique to Colorado, with tall, mostly flat lava-capped plateaus rising high from the valley floor, their dramatic red cliffs dropping steeply downward. Glaciers from several thousand years ago left many valleys and lakes evident throughout this wilderness. If you are looking for gorgeous lakes with multiple choices for good fishing on a less-traveled trail, with the option to climb up to a high mountain pass overlooking the Flat Tops with incredible views, look no farther. This trail will be more dry and passable in late summer or early fall, which is when I recommend doing this hike, and there will be fewer mosquitos, as the Flat Tops can be inundated with them during the summer months. The trail is very well maintained as it skirts by Mud Mandall, Twin Mandall, and Slide Mandall Lakes, all the way up to Black Mandall Lake; a little over 4.0 miles. If you decide to hike the additional 1.5 miles to the pass after reaching Black Mandall Lake, please note that the trail becomes faint and then nonexistent for a significant section. There are some rock cairns and make-

Black Mandall Lake looking south toward Flat Top Mountain.

shift posts in the area to help guide you, but you must pay attention nonetheless because it can be easy to get off track. The trail does become more obvious again as you make the final push up a rocky segment to the pass. Also, be prepared for high winds and turbulent weather and understand that after you are above tree line, there is no shelter. I think you'll find the views and adventure worth it.

GETTING THERE: From Steamboat Springs, drive south on US Highway 40 for just more than 3.5 miles, then turn right (south) on State Highway 131 towards the small town of Yampa. At Yampa, turn right at Main Street; there is a gas station here for reference. Drive through town, and at the end of the road turn left on County Road 7. Follow this road for about 12.4 miles or so to the trailhead. (This road turns into dirt and becomes FSR 900 after a few miles.) You will climb up to and then circle the large Yamcolo Reservoir. Shortly after, you will see Bear Lake Campground on your left, and just a little farther past that, you will see a sign for Mandall Creek on your right—it's easy to miss, though. There will be a small parking area on your left. Park here. The parking lot overlooks Flat Top Mountain and Upper Stillwater Reservoir, also called the Yampa Reservoir. It can also be referred to as Bear Lake, depending on which map you use.

THE ROUTE: The trailhead is on the north side of the road where you parked. Cross the road and climb up the obvious trail into the trees, and then you will see the trailhead map and register. The initial climb will zigzag steeply up through aspen trees, providing glimpses here and there of Flat Top Mountain and Derby Peak to the south. At 0.8 mile you will reach the Flat Tops Wilderness boundary, marked with a sign. If you look closely, you will see an old faint trail to the left, obviously blocked off with large logs. This is the old trail, which had to be rerouted back in 2001 because of a large landslide, and many maps still show it as being the correct route. Do not go in that direction, but instead continue up the obvious trail to the right of this wilderness sign, climbing farther up some steep slopes before crossing a small creek.

The Engelmann spruce and subalpine fir here provide a nice canopy of shade as you approach a spur trail to the right that leads down to a small pond at about 1.5 miles. Continue past the pond, eventually working your way down and around, passing another small stand of aspen just before reaching a large, open meadow. At around 2.0 miles you will pass by the old section of trail that had to be

Slide Mandall Lake.

rerouted; stay to the right here and continue in a northwesterly direction. The views from this meadow are fantastic because now Mandall Pass is clearly visible to the northwest, with Flat Top Mountain standing proud to the south.

The sound of Mandall Creek will become louder before you soon have to cross it. There was a somewhat flat log there to assist, but who knows how long it will remain before it has to be replaced. The trail continues up with smaller creek crossings here and there. At times, the trail seems to be a double track; perhaps it is from the runoff choosing to take the path of least resistance, tempting hikers to hike alongside it and thus creating a secondary trail. In any case, it's not too confusing—just use the most durable path. I really enjoy this segment of trail because the cliffs of the mountains become more prominent the farther up you hike.

At around 3.2 miles, you will see a faint spur trail to the left; this is the path that leads to Slide Mandall Lake, a nice place to stop for a break or for fishing. Please note no camping or fires are allowed within 100 feet of this lake. After exploring Slide Mandall, continue back on the main trail, continuing northwest. You will reach a patch of willows to cross. There is a bridge, but it is not in the best shape; many planks are missing, and the wood seems to be rotting, so use caution here as you cross.

Just before reaching the Black Mandall Lake spur trail, you will come to a pond where it appears the trail crosses this pond; it doesn't. Look for the trail as it goes to the right, around this pond. It's easy enough to backtrack if you missed it, and it becomes much more evident on your return trip. The trail climbs up just a little farther before reaching the cutoff for the Black Mandall Lake Trail. Going right takes you to the lake, an easy 0.25 mile. At just over 4.0 miles, you have reached the shore of Black Mandall Lake. Take in the views, perhaps have some lunch, and retrace your steps back to the main trail, #1121.

Going left at the main trail will take you back to the trailhead. When you reach that large meadow on your return trip, remember not to hike on the old, rerouted trail, but turn left at the fork to return the way you came. If you'd like to continue up to Mandall Pass, take a right at the fork after leaving Black Mandall Lake and read on.

Continue north on Trail #1121 through meadows and forest; at about 0.7 mile, you will notice the trail starts to fade as you exit tree line. From this point on it's important to keep your eyes on the horizon for old trail markers (wooden posts sticking out of rock cairns); these will help guide you up and across a very large meadow, with Mandall Pass glaringly obvious above. There are several of these markers, somewhat in opposition to "Leave No Trace" ethics, but I found them quite reassuring until the trail became obvious again. The main rule is to hike north across the large meadow toward the rocks just below the scree field in front of you. The meadow will be marshy and quite possibly too soggy if you hike too early in the season.

Continue past a few more rock cairns near the scree field, and before you know it, the trail becomes visible again, winding its way up steeply. There are several nice flat spots to stop and take a picture, or catch your breath, as I had to do. Expect to see some remaining snowfields along the way as well. You'll know you've reached the pass after the trail levels off. A large rock cairn also marks the trail junction; the faint trail leading east goes up to Orno Peak. The faint trail that heads up near the cliffs to the west is actually an old extension of the trail you just hiked, though it is not well maintained; it eventually heads south and connects with the Devil's Causeway Trail. There are lots of rocks to rest upon at the pass. Sit down for a while, and maybe you'll see a pica or a pair of ptarmigan, as I did. Return the way you came, using caution as you descend the rocky trail, and relish the views of Flat Top Mountain along the way.

MANDALL LAKES TRAIL/MANDALL PASS 99

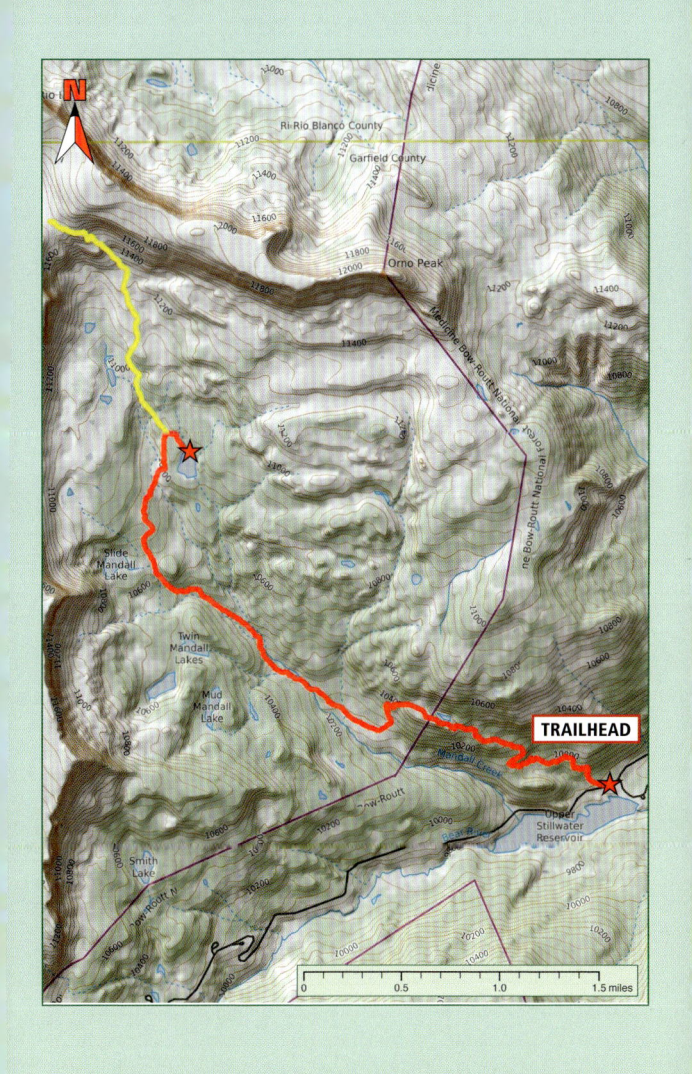

20. Flat Top Mountain

RATING	Difficult
ROUND-TRIP DISTANCE	9.2 miles
ELEVATION GAIN	2,400 feet
ROUND-TRIP TIME	5 hours
MAPS	Trails Illustrated #150 Flat Tops North
NEAREST LANDMARK	Stillwater Reservoir

COMMENT: The Flat Top Mountains were formed slowly over time through glaciation and volcanic activity, the lava caps giving them their erosion-resistant tops, often flat like tabletops. Flat Top Mountain and its neighbor to the southeast, Dome Peak, are easy to see on any given clear day from many of the other trails in this book. To me, there are no better mountains than these to describe exactly what the Flat Tops are: incredibly vast mountains that tower over others despite not having the tall, ragged peaks we normally think of when describing any other Colorado mountain. The Flat Top Mountain summit is at 12,354 feet, the 2-mile bench to the summit clearly visible from the Devil's Causeway and Mandall Lakes Trails.

I gave this trail a rating of difficult as a result of the elevation and exposure because after you crest the saddle below Derby Peak and begin the ascent up the plateau, the trees become nonexistent and the trail fades considerably before disappearing altogether. Expect wind up here, and lots of it. That being said, there are cairns marking the route all along the way, with an obvious cliff band on one side that keeps you from getting off track. There are 360-degree views from the top, and on a good day, you can see for miles and miles in almost any direction.

Snow-dusted Flat Top Mountain as seen from Mandall Lakes Trail.

GETTING THERE: Getting to the trailhead is the same as described for the Devil's Causeway Trail. From Steamboat Springs, drive south on US Highway 40 for just more than 3.5 miles, then turn right (south) on State Highway 131 to the small town of Yampa. At Yampa, turn right at Main Street; there is a gas station here for reference. Drive through town, and at the end of the road turn left on County Road 7 and continue up the road for about 17.0 miles. CR 7 turns into FSR 900 (Bear River Road) just about where the pavement ends. Along the way you will pass Yamcolo Reservoir, then Upper Stillwater (Yampa) Reservoir, and numerous designated camping sites and campgrounds. At the end of the road, park here. There is a large turnaround as well as pit restrooms. Expect the lot to be full on summer weekends. The trailhead sign is just to the left of the restrooms, right next to Stillwater Reservoir (not to be confused with Upper Stillwater Reservoir, which you already drove past).

THE ROUTE: At the reservoir, you will see the trailhead sign for trails #1119, #1120 and #1122. Take a left onto #1122, the Derby Trail. You will stay on the Derby Trail for 2.2 miles before turning left (northeast) to make the final 2-plus-mile trek up to the summit of Flat Top Mountain. At the start of the hike, the trail crosses the dam on the northeast side of the reservoir and then meanders southwest for a short while above the water before turning abruptly southeast and away from the lake. You will see a sign here to let you know you are on the right path. At about 0.4 mile, you will see the trailhead register; sign in here and then continue up the trail. This section is pleasant as you pass a few small ponds and flowery meadows, with Flat Top Mountain towering above; the high bench you will be hiking is clearly visible from here.

At just more than 1.0 mile, you will cross a rather large meadow, again with views of Flat Top Mountain to your left and Derby Peak to the right, with the saddle you will crest between them. The path from here is shady, and for a while, there will be a babbling creek on your right before you begin the steeper ascent to the saddle. The switchbacks will take a little sting out of the elevation gain as you work your way up, but careful footing is required. Take a break at one of the switchbacks and look back down toward the reservoir; the views of Devil's Causeway and the reservoirs are subtle but breathtaking. Cross one more small meadow, and then begin your final push to the saddle. Notice how this final set of switchbacks gives way to shorter trees and bigger views.

At 2.2 miles, you have reached the saddle. You are halfway there. This is a good place to take a break, reassess the weather, and refuel for the big push to the summit. From here it can be quite gusty—no trees to provide shelter. There is no sign pointing the way to Flat Top Mountain, but from this point the trail is still obvious. Go left (east by northeast), leaving trail #1122 and continuing up another obvious, though unmarked, trail. You are now on the flank of Flat Top

Derby Peak and Hooper Lake as seen from the shoulder of Flat Top Mountain.

Mountain, with cliffs to your left (north) that keep you from getting off track. (You will hug these cliffs for more than 2.0 miles until you reach the summit.)

At about 0.5 mile after turning off the main trail at the saddle, you will see your first rock cairn even though the trail is still visible. From here the trail becomes faint and then nonexistent for the rest of the way. I found that the best way to stay on track is to stay close to the cliffs, not venturing too far southeast into the alpine tundra. There are also numerous rock cairns to help guide you to the top; I counted at least a dozen, and most of the time they were to my right. If you don't see any, you are probably too far right up the shoulder; hike closer to the cliffs to get back on track. When I hiked this in mid-July, the tundra was alive with small flowers and grasses. Take care to disperse if hiking in a larger group; step on rocks when you can to minimize the impact to this fragile ecosystem.

The long, long bench of Flat Top Mountain leading to the summit.

The final push to the summit entails careful footing as the volcanic basalt rocks become more evident on the tundra until finally, near the summit, you are hiking entirely on rocks. The summit marker is just to the south of a very large cairn where the summit register resides. Bring your own pencil and paper in case the summit register has none because this was what I encountered. Descend the way you came, this time keeping the cliff band to your right, looking for the rock cairns on your left all the way back down to the saddle, then turning right (northeast) back onto trail #1122, the Derby Trail. Follow this back down the way you came, and celebrate back at the parking lot, with memories of Flat Top Mountain and the views forever etched in your mind.

TRAILHEAD

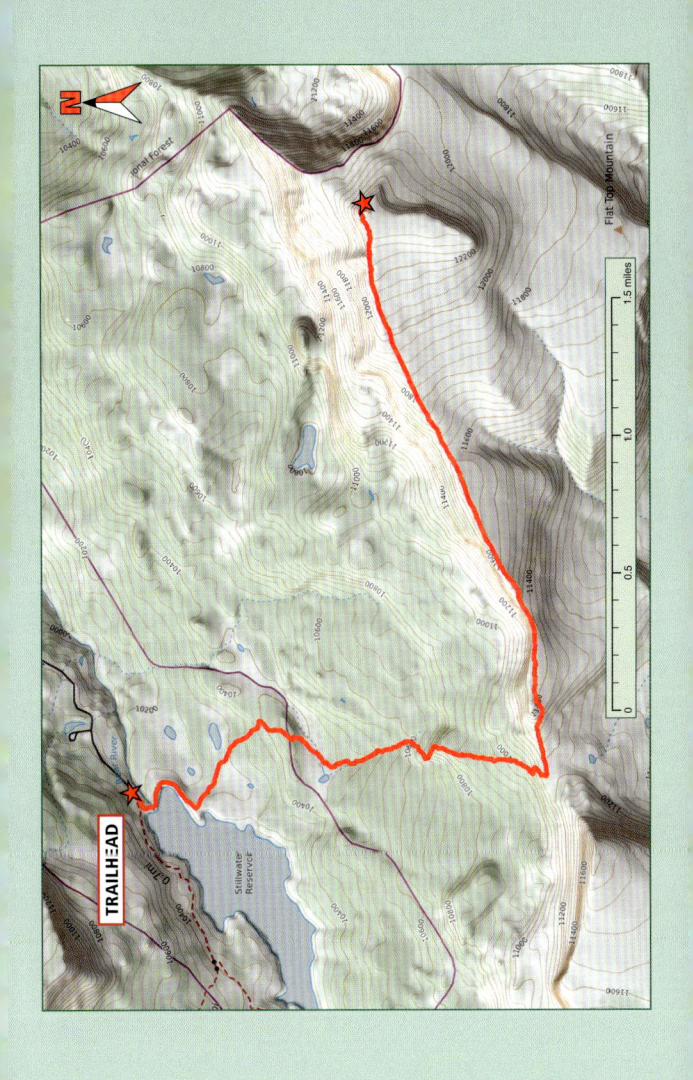

FLAT TOP MOUNTAIN

About the Author

Jacquelyne Cox, known as Jax to many, has lived in Colorado for 25 years. She took her first solo camping and hiking trip in 1996, borrowing a roommate's leaky tent and clumpy sleeping bag. With nothing more than her dog, a map, a few Mexican blankets, and a cooler full of "provisions," she headed straight into the woods northwest of Steamboat. It was during that time, after gazing into the Colorado sky for many hours one night, that she knew she found her place, and that nature was her passion. Although work for the next 20 years kept her from living there, in the back of her mind she knew that someday she would be back.

Jax has traveled all across the Rocky Mountains and beyond as a sales representative for many technical outdoor and ski brands and is fortunate that through her work she was able to foster her love for the great outdoors. From hiking boots and climbing gear to trekking poles, backpacks, and tents to skis and crampons and beyond, Jax has a knack for all things technical, and she proudly "geeks out" when introducing newcomers to innovative gear.

In 2016, at the ripe age of 42, Jax finally reached her goal of 100 days of skiing in a season for the first time in her life—116, to be exact. She is currently plotting her next adventure of mountain biking 100 days in a season, with some fly-fishing and photography adventures tossed in for good measure. She lives with her Alaskan husky, Üllr, named after the Norse god of snow, just south of Steamboat Springs.

Checklist

☐	Hike 1	Hahns Peak	14
☐	Hike 2	Mica Basin	18
☐	Hike 3	Gold Creek Lake/Zirkel Circle	24
☐	Hike 4	Gilpin Lake	30
☐	Hike 5	Three Island Lake	34
☐	Hike 6	Hinman Lake	38
☐	Hike 7	Mad Creek and Saddle Trail	42
☐	Hike 8	Strawberry Park Hot Springs Hike	46
☐	Hike 9	Soda Creek	50
☐	Hike 10	Grizzly Lake	54
☐	Hike 11	Emerald Mountain Quarry/Blackmere	58
☐	Hike 12	Spring Creek	62
☐	Hike 13	Uranium Mine	66
☐	Hike 14	Fish Creek Falls/Upper Fish Creek Falls	70
☐	Hike 15	Thunderhead Trail	74
☐	Hike 16	Rabbit Ears Peak	78
☐	Hike 17	Sarvis Creek	82
☐	Hike 18	Devil's Causeway	88
☐	Hike 19	Mandall Lakes Trail/Mandall Pass	94
☐	Hike 20	Flat Top Mountain	100

Illustration by Jesse Crock

Join Today.
Adventure Tomorrow.

The Colorado Mountain Club helps you maximize living in an outdoor playground and connects you with other adventure-loving mountaineers. We summit 14ers, climbs rock faces, work to protect the mountain experience, and educate generations of Coloradans.

Visit cmc.org/readerspecials
for great membership offers to our readers.